I0416026

By Malang Maane

Self- publishing, book Printing and Publishing Online- Lulu

Designed by Malang Maane.

Printed in the United States of America.

ISBN: 5 800114 551611

This book is dedicated to the thousands of migrants who lost their lives making the treacherous journey across the Mediterranean in search of better lives.

INTRODUCTION

Established in 1951, The International Organization of Migration (IOM) is the leading inter-governmental organization in the field of migration and works closely with Governmental, Intergovernmental and Non-Governmental partners.

According to the IOM, over five thousand migrants lost their lives in 2014 and 2015 making the treacherous journey across the Mediterranean from Libya to start a new life in Europe. This journey which spans from The Gambia (different starting points but this story is being explored from The Gambia as a starting point) across several African nations and finally through Libya and across the Mediterranean to Italy is commonly known in The Gambia as the "Back Way". Italy is usually not the final destination but serves as a way point to other European destinations for most of the "Back Wayers".

The purpose of this book is to give the reader an understanding of the current migrant crisis; the worst since world war II. The true story is that of a young man named Omar from The Gambia who decided to embark on this "Back Way" journey to Europe in search of greener pastures.

The statistics provided by the IOM along with testimonials of those that tackled the journey will undoubtedly paint a picture for you. Wondering what happens next to this young man as you read through this book will make it tough to stop reading.

Have no doubt that upon reading this book you may never take anything for granted again. The ultimate aim of this book is that the reader will be able to save lives by educating friends, family members and the community especially the at-risk populations about the dangers of the "Back Way".

CHAPTER 1

The Gambia is the smallest country on mainland Africa. It is in West Africa, mostly surrounded by Senegal with a short strip of its coastline bordered with the Atlantic Ocean at its western end.

The Gambia, is divided into two long strips by the River Gambia, the nation's name sake, which flows through the center of The Gambia and empties into the Atlantic Ocean. Its area is 10,689 square kilometers (4,127 sq. mi) with a population of 1,882,450 at the 15 April 2013 Census. Banjul is The Gambian capital; with the largest cities being Serekunda and Brikama.

Omar, a 27 year old Gambian, finished high school in The Gambia and was unable to proceed to the University due to an inability to afford the university fees. Omar's father had 18 children and found it difficult to adequately support the family. After high school, Omar started working as a mobile phone technician and made just enough money every month to simply get by. He knew that he had to leave The Gambia to "make it". "Making it" could simply be defined as exiting The Gambia and living a semi-comfortable life overseas. In order to help his family escape their current financial situation, he saw the need to make more money but saw no available opportunity in The Gambia to accomplish that.

The "Back Way" has now become a major topic in The Gambia especially among youths. This topic is widely discussed in all youth gatherings around town, in barbershops, "Attaya" (popular green tea in The Gambia) gatherings, car parks, football fields etc.

One day while at a gathering with his friends, the "Back Way" topic came up as it often did during their hangout sessions. Omar had pondered on this journey many times before and that day was no exception. At the back of his mind, he wondered if this was a journey he could and should embark on. He knew that it could help his situation and give him the means to help his family but he also knew of so many that embarked on the journey but did not make it to their final destination; most perishing in the Mediterranean Sea or in the desert. He had prayed at their funerals after their boats capsized or their smugglers stranded them in the desert; solemn ceremonies with mourners but no bodies.

As that day's conversation proceeded, he got more and more convinced that he could embark on the journey. "Europe is all about luck", said one of his friends. Another friend reminded them that an old hangout buddy, Sulayman, made it through to Italy via the "Back Way". He was now working in a factory in Italy, where the economy was booming, and authorities looked the other way when men arrived from Africa to work.

Sulayman was able to send between $200 and $300 home, a month — sometimes, as much as $450(D20250). His family tore down their home with its thatched roof and built two large, rectangular buildings out of concrete.

The statement, "Europe is all about luck", as well as Sulayman's story, resonated well with Omar and he made the decision to take on the journey. He reasoned with himself and came up with many reasons about going to Europe through the Back Way; some plausible, others not so plausible. His main reason for wanting to leave was to make a better life for himself and support his family. His job as a mobile phone technician in The Gambia was not generating sufficient revenue for him to support himself and help his father support the family and he felt there just seemed no future for him in The Gambia.

> "The burden on a man to provide is a big responsibility, one that cannot be avoided. In The Gambia, It's different for women. They get married and are cared for by their husbands. Men, on the other hand, have to get good jobs, work and support their families" said Omar.

According to the IOM, as of 2014, there were 232 million people around the world who live outside their country of birth. For many of these people, migration means the opportunity for a better life for themselves and their families. Yet, for many others, the search for such an opportunity comes at an extremely high cost, as they face unimaginable and often fatal dangers along their journeys. Some are ready to spend their lifetime savings or take on massive debts and risk their lives and the lives of their families for a new start. Death is a risk worth taking in desperate situations of violence, persecution, famine or even the absence of prospects of a decent life. Migration for a decent life is as old as the human race itself and is the driving force behind much of our history. The unfortunate truth is that most emigrants never find the better life they seek. When someone chooses to migrate in search of a better life, some questions are worth considering. What is a better life? A life where you do not see your friends and family for years at times? A life that usually involves making mediocre living and not utilizing your skills and training? A life that is determined by what you can send back home? Is the better life for you or for your family back home? Does money equal a better life?

> Joaquim Oliveira Martins (Head of the OECD Regional Development Policy Division) says –
> "Better lives means being able to access jobs and income, environmental quality and a good social environment in the places where people live. Insofar as these three dimensions will remain largely disconnected across space, well-being will also remain an average concept with limited impact on individual people's lives."

The "Back Way" has now become one of those unimaginable and often fatal journeys in The Gambia and has seen innumerable casualties but it is still being undertaken by people in large numbers. This avenue of making it to Europe has become the way of choice for many Gambians who are usually at their most productive ages. The reasons for this avenue include lack of affordability of the "right way" and the inability to meet minimum visa requirements.

The "Back Way" journey is not a straight route and has no itineraries, reservations or layovers in airport hotels. There is no refund and no 'satisfaction-guarantees' on the money you gamble to embark on the journey. A "Back Wayer" ends up paying thousands of dollars to be transported from point A to B even if B means the bottom of the ocean. The "Back Way" is nothing new. The term may be new but the route across the Sahara in hopes of making it to Europe has been in effect for decades, albeit not as prevalent as it is nowadays especially among Gambians. One way to look at the issues of the "Back Way" is in the context of European migration policies which have become more restrictive of late. Another way to look at is in in the context of globalization. Three things have changed since the 1980s and could very well be responsible for the "Back Way". The first is that the Gambia's per capita GDP have diverged. In fact, between 1980 and 2000, Africa's average per capita growth rate was zero. The second thing is the large income gap and a greater awareness of it since the 1980s. The "Back Wayers" today know much better the difference in living conditions they can expect in the rich world compared to The Gambia. The third change is the cost of transportation which is definitely not negligible.

The notion that the West is paved with Gold and that the only way to "make it" is to leave The Gambia has led many youths to attempt this treacherous journey.

Many of those that attempt this journey are only able to afford one leg of it at a time and spend months in some of these transits (Mali, Burkina, Niger or Libya) to work and gather more money to resume the journey. The price list as seen at the transport international bus station in Banjul, The Gambia as of May 2015 shows the fare from Banjul to Agadez as D5,000($125). Agadez, Niger is a desert city and the major transit point for "Back Wayers".

Upon completion of school, a vast majority of the youth in The Gambia believe there is no way to make it in there. They harbor the long felt sentiment that they have no future in The Gambia. Stories about how others have gone the "Back Way" and are now living in Europe continue to surface through social media and other outlets. In most cases, the real details of this perilous journey are not given or elaborated on. Photos posted on Facebook and other social media outlets of the "Back Wayers" that successfully completed the journey while awaiting the next steps entice the youths and they yearn to be like these "Back Wayers." There are several reasons why people embark on this treacherous journey from Africa to Europe, risking death along the way. Undoubtedly, for someone to embark on such a risky journey, the reason has to be a profound one.

The Gambia has a liberal, market-based economy characterized by traditional subsistence agriculture, a historic reliance on groundnuts (peanuts) for export earnings. A fluctuating exchange rate with no exchange controls, and a significant tourism industry.

The Gambia's economy is dominated by farming, fishing, and tourism. About a third of the population lives below the international poverty line of US$1.25(D56) a day. Speculatively, there are some families who cannot afford more than one square meal a day.

Is this kind of abject poverty a reason for the "Back Way"?

There are so many stories on social media about "Back Wayers" that have "made it". Is it simply because of envy of these "Back Wayers" and the desire to be like them without understanding the consequences? Is it lack of employment? Could it be due to not having anything to do after finishing school and consequently blending in with idle masses? Are they not interested in entering the university system of The Gambia or do they lack the minimum entry requirements or are unable to afford it? Do they see it as just another dead end? Is it because they consider some jobs too meagre or beneath them? Is it because of pressure from parents? Is the notion that "If you had a relative in the West, you were rich and if not, you remained stuck on the edge of survival" a reason? So many questions, few answers, but the truth remains that the desire to leave The Gambia is now more than ever, very real!

The Gambia gained independence from the United Kingdom on February 18th 1965. Since gaining independence, The Gambia has had two leaders - Dawda Jawara, who ruled from 1970 until 1994, when the current leader His Excellency Alh. Yahya AJJ Jammeh seized power in a coup as a young patriotic army officer.

His Excellency Alh. Yahya AJJ Jammeh addressed migration issues on the international level during the 69th United Nations General Assembly, in New York City, on September 24, 2014.

He voiced concerns over the fact that young and healthy Gambian men and women continue to embark on the hazardous and perilous journey to Europe with all ramifications not only to themselves and their families but also to The Gambia's socio-economic development.

He stressed the fact that in recognition of The Gambia's youth demographic phenomenon, the government of The Gambia in pursuance of its national development goals and priorities has over the years developed several projects and programs to address the situation and hopefully reverse the trend. These include creating greater opportunities for skills acquisition and employment, creation of an enabling environment for job creation amongst others.

Some of these targeted programs include the creation of the National Youth Service Scheme (NYSS), The Gambia Priority Employment Program (GAMJOBS), the Green Industries and "The Campaign against Rural Urban Drift." Some of these national interventions could not be sustained due to a number of factors.

In conclusion, he indicated their expectation of a flexible and swift implementation of projects to create opportunities that will ensure that their youths can take conscious decisions to stay at home and participate meaningfully to bring about the socio-economic advancement of their nation and continent.

The desire to leave The Gambia is not new as the eighties and nineties had seen their fair share. Back then, many focused on applying for schools overseas and hoped for scholarships and parental assistance and guidance. The energy was channeled on what schools to apply; schools that were known for issuing I-20s rapidly. A Form I-20 is the government form that Universities in the United States use to certify to the U.S. government that a prospective student is eligible for F-1 student visa status. One must be accepted as full time student before the form I-20 is issued. Back then, obtaining a visa was not nearly as difficult as it is today. I-20s facilitated the visa process and many were able to get visas. Children from affluent families had no problem obtaining the required application fees for universities abroad and ended up securing colleges and ultimately visas. Some left The Gambia promptly after finishing high school and in some cases even before the O 'level results were released. . O 'levels or Ordinary level was the standard exam at the time issued by the West African Exams Council (WAEC) for form 5. Others had to go on to the 6th form for two more years to do the A 'levels (Advanced level Exam). There were no universities in The Gambia at that time which meant that for those interested in post-secondary education, leaving The Gambia was a must. A few obtained government scholarships and went to Universities in other African nations primarily Sierra Leone, Ghana and Nigeria. A vast majority did not leave and ended up doing other things in The Gambia. Most of those that went to college in other African nations ultimately came back home and now hold notable positions, primarily in the Government. The same cannot be said for those that studied in the West as a good majority never returned upon completion of their studies. Speculatively, so many that went to the West never stepped foot in any college campus. Some of those that stayed behind acquired jobs and others entered into businesses and later traveled for greener pastures. Many wondered why they were not afforded the opportunity to travel. Perhaps if the "Back Way" was a widely known option back then some may have entertained it. The eighties and nineties was also an era of "semesters". Semester is a slang widely used in The Gambia for folks holidaying there after being overseas. This was an era that traveling overseas was not as prevalent as it is now and hence these semesters were easily noticed. Common among semesters back then were dreadlocks which made for easy identification. Their dreadlocks, jewelry, fancy vehicles and lavish spending made them stand out. The manner in which their wealth in Europe was gathered was a speculative subject and left many wondering how so much wealth was acquired in such a small amount of time. The manner in which their wealth was attained, however, did not appear to be an issue to most as the aspirations of being a semester grew stronger and deeper. The youth simply wanted to be like these semesters. Despite all the speculations about how so many became so rich quickly, they remained the envy of most. This goes further to drive the point home that poverty is a crime and some accept and embrace 'rich' people regardless of the reason surrounding the accumulation of their 'wealth'. Almost synonymous to the celebrity fever that currently plagues the US. A lot of people want to be celebrities!

So many people, especially the youth were quite impressed by the "semesters" and even more amazed at how quickly they became rich after leaving The Gambia for Europe. No one, however, can be naïve to the fact that to every get rich quick scheme there are usually serious, sometimes fatal consequences behind it. Some youths on the other hand were not impressed by the "semesters". They were not interested in going to Germany which was the main destination for the "semesters" at the time. Their interest was going to America and living the American Dream. They wanted to go to America, study and promptly come back home to help their nation, supposedly. For a lot of those that made it to America, as it turned out, did not return promptly after finishing their studies for a variety of reasons- reasons that are out of the scope of this book.

It is very safe to assume that the semester era has now metamorphosed into the "Back Way". The ultimate goal of most "Back Wayers" is to be a semester and to "make it". Most want to come back home and showcase their 'wealth' or just live a comfortable life with their families. One of the differences between the "semester" and the "Back Wayer", of course, is the method of getting overseas; the "Back Way" versus a plane ride. The current difficulty in obtaining visas to the west coupled with the porous nature of Libyan borders have probably giant leaped the number of "Back Wayers". It is amazing and perhaps disheartening that despite the fact that the statistics are stacked up heavily against the "Back Way" journey coupled with the uncertainties that lie ahead while in Europe, the "Back Wayers" are more determined now than ever to undertake this journey. It is not a secret that so many people that embark on this journey never live to fulfil their dreams. It is a common knowledge that so many parents dealt with the demise of their kids and are not even afforded the opportunity of viewing their sons' or daughters' bodies; Bodies that have perished in the Mediterranean Sea or in the Sahara Desert. A tragedy indeed!

Up until the early 1990s, Gambians did not need visas to enter England in the United Kingdom. Consequently, this made it easier for any Gambian who wanted to travel and who could afford the airfare and arrange for accommodation from friends and relatives in the UK. Once in England, many ventured into other European nations that were more appealing to the "semester" cause. It was an era where the unfortunate went to UK on Tuesday and were back on Friday because they were refused entry. The introduction of the need for a visa could be seen as a good thing in that one does not have to travel to the UK wondering if he or she will be allowed entry. This has eliminated the money wasted in traveling to the UK simply to be refused entry for whatever reason. With a Visa on your passport, one is almost guaranteed an entry thereby eliminating the uncertainties that plagued the 'no visa required' era.

Before the "Back Way" and perhaps not as common was stowaway. This was another avenue of entering the West illegally by hiding aboard a vehicle, ship or aircraft to gain free passage. There was a story about how in a desperate ploy to reach a better life in Europe, a man from

Guinea Conakry, West Africa was arrested at the border between Morocco and Ceuta. He was trying to smuggle himself into Europe by wedging himself in a tiny space behind the car's engine. He was found lying in a fetal position having choked on petrol fumes. Another story was that of two young African stowaways who were found dead in the landing gear of a plane in Brussels. They left a handwritten letter explaining the hardships that caused them to pursue such an incredulous plan. The two thought they had prepared carefully for their trip, each donning several pairs of trousers, pullovers and jackets. However, those along with their plastic sandals, were woefully inadequate to save them in high-altitude temperatures of -55C.

It is not the boys' death which was shocking but the fact that the letter found wrapped in their clothing, showed that they quite expected to die in their attempt to escape and at the same time making a plea for Europe to help the young people of Africa.

Africa has never seen such a flood of young men heading for Europe. The number of migrants crossing by sea to Italy, a top entry point, nearly quadrupled from 2013 to 2014, reaching about 170,100. Sub-Saharan Africans made up a growing percentage of the total, with around 64,600 arriving last year. This year (2015), the figure is expected to be even higher. The Gambia, one of Africa's smallest nations, is a big contributor to that flow.

It is easy to conclude that this journey across the Mediterranean qualifies as mass exodus. What is responsible for the mass exodus?

Why are Gambians so desperate and determined to reach Europe by any means necessary? Are conditions so deplorable in The Gambia that folks want to leave and take all the risks that come along with undertaking this journey? Could the case be made that the efforts of the European Union (EU) and the North Atlantic Treaty Organization (NATO) military intervention 'to protect' the Libyan people and thereby rendering the nation's borders porous, according to those against the intervention, be a reason?

Children finish school either by dropping out or simply concluding the highest level of education they can before post-secondary. There is a university in The Gambia which has seen thousands graduate since its inception. The reason why many are not swayed by attempting to go to college/university in The Gambia is undoubtedly a speculative subject. From back in the eighties, leaving The Gambia after high school was the norm for those that were able and it appears that the phenomenon has not changed. One wonders why trying to get skilled in something and achieving viable employment does not cross the mind of the would-be "Back Wayer" or the masses as a whole. A long held attitude for many is that one just cannot succeed in The Gambia. For those that retain this sentiment, comes the notion that they absolutely must exit The Gambia to be successful. They have to exit the smiling coast of Africa to "make it". The exit strategies, unfortunately include the "Back Way" and rarely the "right" way; in a seat on a plane. This is an Era that securing a visa to travel overseas is almost non-existent and for many, a thing of the past. So quite naturally the time, dedication, effort and money required to secure a visa does not resonate well with the would-be "Back Wayer".

So with justifiable reasons, he does not even want to entertain the idea of going through this timely process. This is simply viewed as just a futile attempt and generally categorized as a mere waste of time. Instead of trying to create opportunities where there seem to be none, instead of persistently looking for alternatives of "making it", the "Back Way" is rather seen as the only option of alleviating the hardships encountered in The Gambia. Instead of several thousands of Dalasis as is the case for going to the west the 'right way', the would-be "Back Wayer" only needs to collect as little as D5,000 ($125) to start the journey. This is enough, in most cases, to make it as far as Agadez, Niger, 2300 miles from Banjul. In order to get the required money as well as get his parents' blessing, the would-be "Back Wayer" starts the topic with his parents. Many yearn for help from parents while others find whatever work they can to save up for the route. Most of these parents are struggling themselves and would like nothing better than for their children to "make it" and in turn help them. "The journey is very easy now" one parent said. Of course, this statement is subject to scrutiny as many can argue that there is nothing easy about this journey.

Most of the "Back Wayers" come from similar economic backgrounds that necessitated their desire to embark on the journey. They had mostly been born into financially-strapped families whose situations never improved as the years went by. As young adults, their outlook of life remained quite grim because of the very limited opportunities available to them.

Omar's plan was to talk to his parents to see if they could help him gather the funds required to start the journey. Omar clearly understood how dangerous the journey was. He had heard stories from family members and also on news outlets. He had obtained quite a wealth of information from families and friends of those that have already made the journey. "With social networks, "WhatsApp", "Viber", we can communicate with our friends who are in Europe. They send us photos of their new adoptive parents there, and all of this gives us the appetite to get there and search for more money," said Omar.

Omar's plan was to tackle the journey alone and hoped to meet his fellow countrymen along the way. This is not always the case as the transportation system is unpredictable. He explained how he was told that there are times that you leave with someone but end up not being together. "This is a route that you sometimes stop because you do not have enough money to continue and are left behind. You wait for money to be sent from family so you can continue". Omar explained, based on what he had been informed.

In general the would-be "Back Wayer's" parents engage in conversations, perhaps reluctantly, to determine how to make the journey happen. These parents consult other family members and also parents of previous "Back Wayers" in an attempt to gain knowledge about this "Back Way" journey. Arguably, they want someone to discourage them, someone to deter them from investing in a potentially deadly journey. Nonetheless the reality of it is that they ultimately end up supporting and sponsoring the journey. Many have had to resort to selling properties or using them as collateral to secure the funds needed for the entire journey or part of it. The amount of money needed to furnish the whole trip is usually unknown as there are a lot of variables; variables that include possible kidnappings and ransom required for release. The parents are urged, or perhaps pressured to simply provide only enough to start the journey. It is believed that about D10000 ($250) is needed to start the treacherous journey but the total cost could be well in the thousands of dollars. With the startup money gathered and a lot of prayers, the kids are sent packing into the lands of the unknown. Undoubtedly, these parents care deeply for their children but to see them prosper, they'll do whatever it takes even basically driving them to what may become their demise. A parent of someone that embarked on the journey explained how he just had no choice as his son would have gone either way. He lamented on how he had sleepless nights and prayed for the safe arrival of his son. He explained how after 3 weeks of not hearing from him (the time he spent in the desert), he feared the worst. At the time of his narration, his son had made it to Libya and was awaiting more money in order to continue on to Italy through the Mediterranean. This came on the heels of a tragedy of a boat capsizing in the Mediterranean Sea.

Twice a week, a bus called the "TA Express," full of young men wearing sandals and carrying small bags, leaves Banjul on its way to Agadez, Niger.

Omar was not so sure he could secure the funds for the fare from Banjul to Agadez from his family. He knew he could not save that kind of money. Nonetheless, he decided to talk to his parents. Later that evening, he decided to reveal his plan to his parents.

Both of his parents disagreed with his decision but were very hesitant to admonish him. His father told him that he did not have the funds. He went on to say that had they owned the house they lived in, he would have put it up as collateral. His mother talked to several other family members. Deep down, she was hoping for someone to advice against this perilous journey. As expected, most of those she spoke to were vehemently against this journey. Omar was determined to make it and came up with a different plan. He needed just enough money to make it to Mali. He hoped by the time he got to Mali, his parents would have secured some money to get him to the next phase of the journey. Naturally, this was wishful thinking but for Omar, he had faith and was determined to take on the journey by any means necessary. Over the next few days, he gathered as much information as he could about the journey. On Facebook, he found others that had successfully completed the "Back Way". He saw the nice photos they posted and he yearned to be like them. During interactions with those that went the "Back Way", he was informed of the many checkpoints along the way and advised to get as many ID cards as possible. "The checkpoint officials hang on to your ID card and give it back to you once you pay", he said. "I was told to get as many ID cards as possible", he went on to say. This would help him avoid some of the bribes and simply have these officials hang on to his duplicated ID. Omar was able to get a local printing and laminating shop in town to make him up to 20 copies of his ID. He got a few shirts and also a coat at the Albert market in Banjul. He was told that it gets very cold in the desert. Despite not knowing exactly when he would make it to the desert, he still got the coat just in case. In The Gambia, he was informed of an agent in Senegal.

On October 26th, 2012 after having secured enough money to make it as far as Mali, Omar set out to embark on the treacherous journey. He had approximately D2000 ($50), his back pack with two shirts, a tooth brush, and paste and his Nokia mobile phone. He was to meet with an agent in Senegal. Senegal surrounds The Gambia on 3 sides. In Senegal, this agent will put him in contact with someone in Mali. So, in the middle of the night Omar left Banjul for Dakar, the capital of Senegal. His departure was kept a secret outside of the immediate family for a few days or so following. This was primarily for good luck and also to avoid being discouraged. Very little noise is made about the trip until well after it has begun. His parents prayed for him, wished him luck and saw him off.

The "Back Wayer" has little difficulty leaving The Gambia and entering Senegal, the next logical hub in the journey as this is perhaps the simplest for Gambian citizens. Gambians, like all West Africans, only need an Identification card to enter Senegal.

Omar, after crossing the ferry in Banjul to Barra, continued on his mission to Europe; A mission that will see him go through several African cities. He experienced little resistance from checkpoint security officials along the way from The Gambia all the way into Dakar, the capital of Senegal. The little resistance was removed simply by paying a small bribe, as little as D50 ($1.25).

CHAPTER 2

Senegal has a wide variety of ethnic groups and, as in most West African countries, several languages are widely spoken. The Wollof are the largest single ethnic group in Senegal at 43 percent. Just like in The Gambia, Wollof is widely spoken which makes communication easy for the "Back Wayers" while in Senegal.

Senegal officially the Republic of Senegal is a country in West Africa. It is the westernmost country in the mainland of the Old World or Eurafrasia and owes its name to the Senegal River that borders it to the east and north.

Senegal covers a land area of almost 197,000 square kilometers (76,000 sq. mi), and has an estimated population of about 13 million. The climate is tropical and alternates between a dry season and rainy season. Senegal's capital and largest city is Dakar. The journey to Agadez from Banjul goes through Dakar.

Senegal is externally bounded by the Atlantic Ocean to the west, Mauritania to the north, Mali to the east, Guinea Conakry and Guinea-Bissau to the south. Internally it almost completely surrounds The Gambia, namely on the north, east and south, leaving The Gambia's short Atlantic coastline.

After 5 hours or so, Omar made it to Dakar, October 27th 2012. He had no problems meeting with his agent who promptly showed up after a phone call to pick him up from the bus station. Omar was whisked into a house in the outskirts of Dakar where he was to be briefed and contact made with an agent in Mali. That night, while at that house, he met other "Back Wayers". They all had stories to tell. He was told that several "Back Wayers", while in Senegal have had cold feet or faced tremendous pressure from family back home in The Gambia to abandon the journey and return home. This is a direct result of family members not being aware of a "Back Wayer's" true intention of departing Banjul only to realise it later, usually while the "Back Wayer" was in Senegal.

Because The Gambia is so close to Senegal and also close family relations exist to make a visit plausible, no alarm bells are raised when the would-be "Back Wayer" advises of his intention to travel to Senegal. Needless to say, there are a good number of would-be "Back Wayers'" whose intentions are met with a huge amount of resistance from family and friends. Some of those assuming that they may face resistance from family and friends simply announce their departure to Senegal, knowing no one would really question the reason for the travel. In Senegal, they quickly realize they are not prepared for the journey due to a variety of reasons; lack of funds being the main culprit. In their absence from The Gambia, their true intentions are realized and somehow quickly spread and pressure to return builds up from family members. Some return but others who are determined proceed regardless of any pressure or uncertainties. While in Senegal some lay low as they continue to survey the journey and gather information about it; pertinent information that should have been gathered prior to embarking on the trip. While in Senegal, smuggler connections are initiated and several contacts are made. Unfortunately, some are scammed out of their money and sometimes their documents even while in Senegal forcing them to abort the mission.

Sadibou, Omar's agent in Senegal had been in the business for decades. He told them of a story of Djibi, a man who left Dakar in the nineties to embark on a "Back Way journey" to Europe. Sadibou explained how this journey had been in effect for decades. It is just now that it has become more common.

Djibi left in 1999 hoping to be in Europe by the new millennium. He had been informed that the $1300 (D60000) he paid to an agent in Dakar would cover the entire cost of his transportation. He journeyed by train into Bamako, the capital of Mali which shares a border with Senegal. Upon arrival in Bamako his contact there informed him that he had not been paid. This contact was supposed to have been paid by Djibi's agent in Dakar but somehow that never occurred. He had to call Dakar to arrange for a western union transfer from his wife to pay the agent's contact.

As Omar listened to this story, he started to wonder if Sadibou would deliver his promise. He remained hopeful and continued listening to the story.

In Mali, Djibi encountered a group of Africans who were on the same mission as him. It was in Mali that he learnt of the horrific stories associated with trying to cross the Sahara. He met quite a few Africans who had attempted and decided to abandon the journey and return home. One man had already made it to Cueta, Spain but was deported to the border between Morocco and Algeria. He learnt of stories of Algerian police shooting people on sight in remote areas. He heard of several stories of armed robbers taking the migrants' money and leaving them to die in the desert. Despite being afraid, he decided to continue his mission. He said his mother was terrified and asked him to return but his father told him that he dreamt about him being okay and encouraged him to continue.

Omar wondered why his agent was telling them this story. "Did he want us to abort our mission", he asked himself. Omar did not think anything could make him change his mind and he was confident in the prayers his parents had given him.

In Mali, Djibi met a man who organized a flight for him and other groups of Africans to Timbuktu. Timbuktu is a city in the West African nation of Mali situated 12miles north of the River Niger on the southern edge of the Sahara Desert. Once in Timbuktu, along with fifteen other Africans, they travelled in a truck all night before reaching Gao, Mali which is the last stop before the Desert. It is approximately 200miles east-southeast of Timbuktu. In Gao, they met thousands of other migrants waiting for transportation to cross the Sahara. The travel across the Sahara was conducted mainly at night. He explained how one afternoon the driver stopped to show them the graves of people. They apparently died after their truck broke down and had waited in vain for help before dying of thirst.

During the day, he explained that they would rest under the truck but were sleep deprived because of the suffocating heat. It took them a whole week to cross the Sahara and reach Algeria. Unfortunately for them, in Algeria, they were stopped by Police, beaten and given twenty four hours to leave the country. Their determination to complete the mission at hand made them choose to not heed the order of the Police. They had run out of money but fortunately, one of them had about $5 (D200) on him. They used this money to buy trinkets to sell for a profit and raise enough money to continue their journey. After being in Algeria for three weeks and living in abandoned houses they eventually met a Senegalese man who promised to take them across the border into Morocco.

Three others from the group gave up the journey after being told that they would have to walk 20km through the mountains to Morocco to avoid the official border crossings. He said that they were told that lots of migrants died in these mountains after being deported from Morocco and abandoned. Still, he along with a few of his companions, decided not to give up and walked for 2 days before reaching a village where they caught a bus to Casablanca, Morocco. Casablanca is the largest city in Morocco located in the north western part of the country on the Atlantic Ocean. It is about 1200 miles from Timbuktu, Mali. The entire time since leaving Bamako they had not taken a shower and by this time, their bodies were even covered with fleas and they looked like mad men. In Casablanca, he was able to find work in construction but the pay wasn't enough. He was not able to save enough money to get him across the border and ultimately he had to call home. His wife sold their TV along with other possessions and borrowed money from friends. While waiting at the Western union to collect the $700 (D28000) that his wife was able to secure, he met some Senegalese men who had the same plight as him. Fortunately the Senegalese had a guide who agreed to let him travel with them for $600 (D24000). He explained how on that same night he had a great feeling after going on top of a roof and seeing the lights of the Spanish mainland across the Mediterranean. It was such a wonderful feeling as he figured the end was in sight. "It was an amazing sight; After all I had been through to finally see my destination even though I knew I hadn't reached it yet" he said. Their guide advised them to buy lots of black clothes and told them that at midnight a taxi would pick the three of them along with seven others to take them to the forest near the border of Cueta. He explained how disease spread rapidly in this forest as conditions were so terrible and no water to wash their hands or clean themselves even after going to   the   toilet.

The idea was to try to climb the barbed wire fence that separates Morocco and Cueta. The problem however, was that so many that tried this method of reaching Cueta were caught and severely punished before being sent back. After a week of contemplating climbing over the fence, he was informed of a tunnel that was dug beneath the fence. This was a much better alternative but they were not so lucky making it through the tunnel. After 200m into the tunnel, they were found out and again subjected to beating by the police with their rifles. He suffered a tooth loss during this debacle. Nonetheless, he knew he had to complete the journey and nothing short of crossing the border into Europe was acceptable.

He was at a point where he figured that this was a do or die situation and there was no turning back. His second chance came after another week when their guide took them to the coast and showed them an inflatable raft. They all got in the raft and the guide rowed staying close to the shore to avoid detection. Luckily they arrived on Spanish shores 2 hours later, and avoided police detection. They made it to a Red Cross camp in Cueta where he applied as a refugee from Rwanda. If he'd told them where he actually was from, he would have been sent back. This was the first night in four months that he had a good night sleep. Within three weeks, he was given a residence permit and put on a boat to the Spanish mainland. In Armillia, Spain he worked for a month in the fields to secure enough money for a train ride to Italy to join his cousins. He finally arrived at his final destination in Italy only to find out that the phone number he had for his cousins was not a good number any more. He met two Africans at the train station who took him to a hostel. There were 15 migrants living in a single room and there was no room for him. "I could not believe that after everything I had gone through to reach Europe, this was what the life of an Immigrant was like", he said. He spent an entire year living on a filthy floor and selling African trinkets, lighters and bracelets. After 3 years, he was finally able to get papers after the Italian government announced that they would give residence and work permits to illegal immigrants who had a job.

"If I had to do it all over again, I would have waited until I had enough money to buy a plane ticket to Europe and get a visa", he said.

Omar explained how this story touched his heart.

> "If Djibi could do it, I knew I could and I was determined to do it. I can appreciate Djibi saying that next time he would try to get a visa but I know that was just not an option I had. They just do not grant visas anymore", he said gingerly.

CHAPTER 3

The calculated flying distance from Dakar to Bamako (capital of Mali) is equal to 649 miles which is equal to 1045 km. If you want to go by car, the driving distance between Dakar and Bamako is 1353.45 km. If you ride your car with an average speed of 112 kilometers/hour (70 miles/h), travel time will be 12 hours 05 minutes. As we already know, Omar is neither flying nor driving in his private car so the journey on a bus, van or truck with frequent checkpoints stops could take him well over two days.

The next morning, October 28th 2012, Omar, with the help of his agent boarded a van to Bamako, Mali. He called his parents back in The Gambia and informed them that he was on his way to Mali. His parents prayed for him and wished him the best.

The next stop from Senegal on this "Back Way" journey is Mali. As earlier mentioned, there is a bus that goes from Banjul, The Gambia to Agadez, Niger. A "Back Wayer" mentioned in an interview that he had paid for the entire journey from The Gambia to Agadez not knowing that he was being scammed. Upon arrival in Mali, he was informed by the driver that the bus had reached its final destination. He was forced to find a way to continue the journey.

Omar, was not able to pay for a trip from Banjul to Agadez so for him, Mali was his final destination for now. After two days of being on the road, on October 30th, Omar arrived in Bamako, Mali. Again, he had little difficulty locating his contact. Omar's plan was to find work in Mali so he could continue his mission across the Mediterranean into Italy. While in Mali, his contact there put him in touch with a Gambian who offered to provide him with accommodation while he searched for work. He was very glad to be in a Gambian's house and that night he slept very well.

He again called his family and informed them of his safe arrival in Mali. He told them that he would be in Mali until he could secure more money to continue the journey.

While in Mali, Omar met Lamine, a young man from Mali who told him that his advice for anyone stranded was to simply go back home. He explained his story to Omar.

> "In 2011, I also set off on the long journey to Italy. For the trip to Libya alone, I paid 800,000 CFA francs (about $1400 or D56000). The money was for bus tickets, transport by truck, bribes, accommodation and payment for traffickers. While in Libya, I changed my mind. I stayed there for about four and a half months because I didn't have enough money to pay for the whole trip", explained Lamine.

He went on to say that things did not work out as he had hoped. He was picked up by traffickers, locked up and told he would have to pay for the journey across the Mediterranean.

> "After being mistreated in Libya, I decided to return home to Mali. I was able to make my way to a camp run by the IOM on the outskirts of Agadez", said Lamine.

Returnees can stay at this camp for a few days. The IOM provides accommodation, food, showers and fresh clothing and helps with travel arrangements. Lamine was happy to be there. He eventually made it back to Mali.

Mali lies in the Torrid Zone and is among the hottest countries in the world. Most of the country lies in the southern Sahara Desert which produces an extremely hot, dust-laden Sudanian savanna zone. Mali is landlocked with an area of just over 1,240,000 square kilometers. It is one of the poorest countries in the world. The average worker's annual salary is approximately US$1,500(D60000). Due to this fact, for the "Back Wayer" that is not able to secure enough funds to go past Mali, it may take months working as day laborers among other jobs to secure enough money to continue the journey.

Some "Back Wayers" often find themselves running out of money while in Mali. Unable to pay any more bribes at checkpoints, they have to figure ways of hiding to avoid detention through some of these checkpoints. Fears of their passports being confiscated and not given back become very real especially when they run out of money to pay for any more bribes. Quite a few had to deal with their passports being confiscated and had to call home to have their folks send them money so they can pay up to continue their journey. Some had to return home because of issues with passports being taken away from them coupled with no money left. In some cases they simply realized that the complications of the journey were highly underestimated. Several "Back Wayers" are known to have stayed in Mali where they secured menial jobs to secure money to continue the journey to Agadez.

While in Mali, Omar eventually found work again as a mobile phone technician in the city of Bamako. He continued working for about two months but the pay was so meagre, he could barely earn enough money to sustain himself. He reached out to his parents but as expected they were not in a financial situation to help him. They were happy to hear from him and more importantly to know that he was doing well. They urged him to continue to have faith and that he had their prayers and blessings. "I stayed there for a few months and continued working as a mobile phone technician," he says. "The pay was meagre so I made the decision to move on to find better paid work in Burkina Faso." He had been informed of a small town called Beguedo in Burkina Faso. He was advised that as a mobile phone technician, he should be able to secure work quickly.

CHAPTER 4

Burkina Faso is a landlocked country in West Africa. Burkina, formerly Upper Volta is around 274,200 Sq Km in size and surrounded by Mali to the north among other countries. Its capital, Ouagadougou, is one of the stops of the TA express that leaves from Banjul to Agadez.

As of 2014, the population of Burkina was estimated at just over 17.3 million. The country owes its former name of Upper Volta to three rivers which cross it; the Black Volta, the White Volta and the Red Volta. According to the March 2011 Euromoney Country risk rankings, Burkina Faso was ranked the 111th safest investment destination in the world. Remittances used to be an important source of income to Burkina Faso. But during the 1990s with unrest in the Ivory Coast (the main destination for Burkinabe emigrants), many were forced to return home. Now, remittances account for less than 1% of GDP. Burkina is the fourth largest gold producer in Africa behind South Africa, Mali and Ghana. Transport in Burkina Faso is hampered by largely underdeveloped infrastructure as in a lot of African nations. Only 22.7 percent of the African road network is paved. Although studies show a reduction in official checkpoints along many routes in Burkina and in Africa as a whole, there are increased reports of the vacuum being filled by unofficial checkpoints.

On December 20th 2012, in the middle of the night, Omar was able to hitch hike on the back of a pickup truck from Bamako to Ouagadougou, Burkina Faso. It took him approximately 15hours to complete this journey. Even still, in Burkina, issues of several checkpoints also arise. And again Omar's only way to make it through was simply by bribery.

From Ouagadougou, he was again able to hitch hike his way to his destination of Beguedo, a small village in Burkina Faso, 230km (140 miles) south-east of Ouagadougou. This trip usually takes 3 hours but it took him over 6 hours. He arrived safely in Beguedo on December 22nd 2012.

Beguedo, Burkina Faso is a town where several women live without their husbands. The village is dubbed the town of women. This is due to the unintended consequences of the migrant crises. The unfortunate truth is that Beguedo is not unique as there are many African villages just like it. Husbands and wives are forced to live thousands of miles apart. Many husbands, in search of greener pastures, chose to go the "Back Way" leaving their wives behind. So many wives in Beguedo have not seen their husbands in several years. Most of these husbands are in Italy where they work and try to attain better lives for their families. The women, in most cases, do not even care about the 'better' lives. They simply want their husbands with them. They wonder when they will be reunited with these men.

Up until the early nineties, Burkinabes did not need visas to Italy. So many left for Italy and were able to work hard and send money home. Several nice houses and buildings in Beguedo were built by the "Italians". The migrants in Italy are known as "Italians" back in Beguedo. They were able to build houses for their families. A visa is now required and does not come easy at all in Burkina just like in most African nations. Burkinabes still find a way to make it to Italy, usually through the treacherous journey across the Mediterranean. Unfortunately, Italy is no longer how it used to be. Work is not as abundant as it used to be as the country is going through its own economic crisis. The amount of money they were able to send back home has significantly gone down. The reason is mainly due to the current economic crisis in Italy. Many are not even able to send $25 (D1000) a month.

Wives end up moving in with their in-laws and remain faithful to their husbands. They however have no idea what their husbands are doing overseas. For these wives, what happens in Italy stays in Italy. They simply are not in the know of what their husbands are up to in Italy. The only means of communication with them is through telephones. For those that are fortunate, they get to talk to their husbands once or twice a week. The less fortunate however go months without talking to them. There are stories that these husbands end up marrying Italians. They usually go back home to Beguedo with their Italian wives and introduce their local wives as their relatives. The local wives have 'no' choice but to deal with it. Some of these husbands have documents that allow them to travel back home but they cannot afford the air fare or at least, that's what they say.

When they marry, the husbands promise that they will be back often. They promise to make sure their wives join them in Italy. This is usually not the case. Many of these wives never set foot in Italy. In most cases they end up caring for children who grow up without their fathers. Children, who in many cases, see their fathers once in several years.

There are other stories where the fathers have their older children, and not their mothers, join them in Italy. There are also stories that some of these men return after several years of being in Italy and end up marrying younger women. Again, the wives are told to accept the situation or simply leave. The trend of the men of Beguedo embarking on the "Back Way" and leaving their wives behind continues, sadly. The village continues to be the 'town of women'.

Once in Beguedo, Omar met a nice couple that decided to have him stay with them. They helped him secure a job in town as a mobile phone technician.

While in Beguedo, he met and fell in love with his wife Mary. "She's Christian and I'm Muslim," he says, "but all that matters to us, is that we love each other."

Accepted by her family and after convincing his parents, the couple was married soon after. However, they struggled to make ends meet. Contrary to what Omar was told, the pay as a mobile phone technician was not that lucrative. Still, Omar knew his mission was to make the journey to Europe to search for a better life. His wife Mary, was not going to let him go alone. After all, she is from Beguedo and is all too familiar with the many wives in town who are forced to live without their "Italian" husbands. She made the decision to go with him.

After saving some money from his work as a mobile phone technician in Beguedo, on March 14th, 2013, Omar and Marypaid a truck driver to hide them as they crossed the border from Burkina to Niger.

Once in Niger, Omar and Mary journeyed via bus to Niamey, the capital of Niger. In Niamey, they found several other Africans waiting for their opportunity to get transportation into Libya. The couple along with thirty other people boarded an urban minibus to Agadez. They each paid about $30 (D1200) to the driver. Niamey is 900km from Agadez but the roads are so bad that it takes three to four days to get to Agadez which lies at the edge of the desert.

Omar and Mary encountered several check points by the military police and each time they had to pay their way. "When they see migrants in the bus they say 'stop, out, pay.' If you don't pay they will throw you out of the car", said Omar. On that stretch alone, they paid an additional $30 each on bribes to the checkpoint officials. "Every time the police halts the car, they take our passports and documents and we don't get them back till after paying the bribe", explained Omar. After three days on the road, the couple finally made it to Agadez.

Omar and his wife's ultimate goal was to reach Italy and cross the Mediterranean. They were determined to complete the journey; A journey that goes through Agadez.

By the time they arrived in Agadez on March 17th 2013, all they had were the clothes on their back, along with money for checkpoint bribery and enough for a hotel night stay in the city.

CHAPTER 5

The distance between Agadez, Niger and Ouagadougou, Burkina Faso is approximately 1,143 km which equates to 711miles by plane but over 1400km by road.

Niger is also a landlocked country. It covers a land area of almost 1,270,000km2, making it the largest nation in West Africa. Over 80 percent of its land area is covered by the Sahara Desert. Much of the non-desert portions of the country are threatened by periodic drought and desertification. Agadez is one of the largest cities in Niger with a population of over 78,000. Despite its size, Agadez is sparsely populated.

The general consensus among those who tackled this journey is that going through the desert was the hardest part of the journey. It involved spending several days on the bus from Mali to Agadez with occasional stops at checkpoints to use the bathroom and an opportunity to stretch. While on the bus, they'd talk to each other about what lied ahead; what the next phase of the journey entailed. Sleepless nights as anxiety overtook them night after night. Many wondered if they made the right decision and wondered what their fate would be. A very few contemplated turning back and abandoning the journey but they gathered the strength and encouragement to go on from fellow "Back Wayers". The long wait before they could contact their families back home to advice of their 'safe' arrival in Agadez seemed like it would never end. While on the bus, smuggler contacts are made; the smugglers that will put them on the next phase of their journey. Smugglers whom they had no idea how trustworthy they were. Smugglers that could kidnap them and have them call their families back home for ransom money. A "Back Wayer" commented that it was all about putting your fate in total strangers' hands and simply hoping for the best. "I prayed every opportunity I had, for the best outcome. I convinced myself that it was the right thing to do even though I wondered why I embarked on such a journey. I inevitably started to realize that money is not everything and that my life is not worth losing over wealth or anything for that matter", he said. The "Back Wayers" place their lives and fate in the hands of the smugglers who arrange the next leg of the journey, all the way to the Mediterranean Sea.

"I know all the tricks, how it works from Agadez to Libya", said a man speaking under the condition of anonymity. "When I see that people have the courage to cross the sea, I help them. That's how I earn my living"

"The police are eating too" said another man. Payoffs to corrupt officials, as he gingerly acknowledged, along with the migrants' fierce determination to reach Europe, continue to drive the trade.

Even those at the risk of arrest say that the money that trafficking generates is more powerful than any crackdown on smugglers.

"It's not the real smugglers who get arrested; the real ones are in complicity with the authorities," grumbled a smuggler.

There are so many locations of up and running "ghettos" in town. These are the smuggler locations. They are so many. So many, that you cannot even count them. It is believed that there are over 70 of these "ghettos" in Agadez.

The "Back Wayers" are often abused by the smugglers who abandon them to die in the deserts once they run out of money. The moment their money runs out, they are left behind; Left behind to die in the desert. It is believed that the number of people dying in the desert may be just as staggering as those in the sea.

"It's not just about courage; it's loss of hope", a man exclaimed of the disparaging circumstances driving migrants to leave their homes, families and countries to undertake such a journey to uncertain futures in Europe if they make it that far. "When you lose hope, it's better to try anything" he said, describing himself as the "living dead" and saying that his work was "not a proper job"

"Back there [Senegal], there is absolutely nothing" said a man from Senegal. "We're leaving because we've got to find something for our families. We are with God so we are not afraid. And, we are very tired. We've got to get to Europe", he went on to say.

In Agadez, Omar found work again as a mobile phone technician. Mary frequented the many 'ghettos' in Agadez to figure out how their next phase of the journey would be accomplished. As Omar continued to work to save money, Mary garnered as much info as she could as to how they would make it from Agadez to Libya and ultimately across the

Mediterranean Sea into Italy. In Agadez, Omar met several other Gambians. Many of these Gambians were waiting for their families to send more needed money to allow them to make it to Libya.

It is believed that there are thousands of Gambians stranded in Agadez. There was an article in a Gambian newspaper that described how a lot of Gambians were inhumanely treated by securities, detained and later parked in open trucks and dumped in the desert. It is believed that most of them were beaten and had their monies and other valuables taken from them by armed militia. There are however, camps in Agadez that house most of these stranded Gambians among other migrants. They are vulnerable to attacks as bandits tend to believe they have money and other valuables. For their security, they are asked to stay in the camps. Nonetheless, many claim they are unable to remain endlessly in the camps. They have to enter the main city to make phone calls back to The Gambia as it is a necessity to try to secure funds from their families to resume the journey.

Omar was able to call his family to inform them of his safe arrival in Agadez. He explained to them that he'd met a lot of Gambians stranded in Agadez. His family feared for his safety but as with each phone call, prayed for him and wished him well.

Agadez, a dusty windswept town in northern Niger has long been a crossroad for the Sahara. Sitting on the cusp of the desert's barren landscape, it has now become the final jumping-off point for West African migrants headed to Libya, their sights set on Europe. Fed by an intricate network of smugglers coordinating across West Africa, hundreds stream into Agadez daily by bus, van and private car. Each Monday, as the relentless desert sun begins to arch back towards the horizon, migrants pack into the backs of white Toyota pickup trucks and begin the five-day journey to the Libyan town of Sabha. Smugglers coordinate their departure. They form a loose caravan, in the hopes that traveling in numbers will provide some semblance of safety in the increasingly lawless desert; a desert where hijackings, kidnappings and executions have become one more risk inherent to this already hazardous journey. Rhissou Feltou, the mayor of Agadez says the presence of migrants fuels problems in the town, including crime, drug trafficking and prostitution. "We hear many accounts, quite often that there really are tragedies happening in silence. The EU has a duty to go beyond the seas and explore the issue in its entirety. There's a whole chain that needs help, not only just the Mediterranean but also the desert areas. "The desert has always been a cemetery for immigrants in silence and complete indifference. Travelers tell us they often find bodies- skeletons ravaged by the sands", he said.

In order to make it to Libya and ultimately across the Mediterranean to Italy, the "Back Wayer" inevitably has to go through the Sahara Desert.

After several months in Agadez, Omar and his wife had saved enough money to continue their journey to Libya. They now had to go through the Sahara Desert.

There are Toyota land-cruisers and heavy trucks in Agadez and these are the only cars that can drive through the desert. There are agents that arrange for the trip, of course with a fee. With 30 other people Omar and

Mary got into a Toyota Land-cruiser to start the journey through the desert.

> "If you are less lucky you get into a large truck which takes two hundred people at a time! You stand like sardines in these large trucks and the sun burns you and the desert wind fills your eyes and your mouth and even inside your ears with sand. Whatever type of car it is, it is overloaded and still, some people force themselves to get inside by sitting on the edges or by just jumping and clinging to the car", explained Omar.

After boarding one of two land cruisers to cross the desert, disaster struck.

> "The crossing is very difficult, we knew that we have launched ourselves into a dangerous adventure. It's a bit frightening, but we were going to try to deal with it because in life, you have to be brave. We kept our spirits up along the route so that at the end of the day we could collect the reward," said Omar.

> "We were driving about two kilometers ahead and got a message that the other land cruiser had been stopped by rebels," he went on to say. "They killed the driver, seized the bus and robbed the passengers."

There are no "roads" in the desert and drivers simply follow trails they are familiar with. However, sometimes they miss the trails when there is a desert storm. If a trail is missed everyone dies eventually from heat, exhaustion and dehydration.

Along the route, when the driver gets tired he makes a stop. Omar, Mary along with the other passengers try to get some sleep. The truth however, according to Omar is that one cannot really sleep as it does not make sense to do so.

> "Really to be honest you cannot sleep. We don't feel sleepy because while you sleep anything can happen. People will grab your food and your money if you are not alert. So it is not sensible to sleep, therefore we don't sleep. It is also very cold the more you get into the desert so you could not even sleep if you wanted to", narrated Omar.

Omar and Mary as with the other passengers were each allowed a 7 gallon container with water to drink and some rice. The water containers are tied to the car and hung outside, side by side.

> "Everybody strictly keeps to his own water else there is murder. This water has to last you. When there is a stop you take your tin cup and put some rice in it and eat. Everybody loses weight during this debacle but we stay strong to accomplish our mission" Said Omar boastfully.

Sometimes, these cars break down and that means trouble. Once a breakdown occurs, everyone has to fight for himself to live. One has to get on to another vehicle. A few start walking but the dust covers everything and they panic and easily get lost with the sand everywhere.

"Our car did not break down but another car gave up and we saw people in the desert from that car. We took seven extra people aboard from out of the sand who otherwise would have died. No one knew how they still could fit into our car but they did, they joined our car. The other cars also took as many people as they could. If you did not make it onto a car, you died.
I saw dead people there, and what they do is cover them with some dust and put their passport on top of the heap. This is because someone might pass who knows them and if they do, they take the passport and show it to the relatives", explained Omar.

CHAPTER 6

A journey into the Sahara can be as varied as the desert itself. However there are quintessential Saharan experiences. Most begin in the gateway towns where expeditions out into the desert are organized. Often Oasis, these towns are centres of Saharan culture. In these places, the architecture emerges naturally from the earth and the slow pace of life has changed little in centuries. For exploration beyond the town or village limits, there are two major means of getting around. One, a slow march across the sands astride a camel re-enacts the great camel caravans of Saharan lore. On a camel safari, travelers slow down to a pace well suited to the Sahara's unforgiving climate, allowing you to appreciate the details and pass through this spectacular terrain at one with your surroundings. The other is in a 4WD expedition. Travelers can range further, stirring up the sand as you tick off a list of iconic Saharan landscapes.

Sleeping between four walls is an experience that ends in the towns. Out amid the sands or remote Saharan mountains, evenings are spent around a campfire and a soft bed of sand is the night-time mates of choice. Most Saharan excursions carry tents but many travelers prefer to sleep outdoors beneath the clearest show of stars on earth.

Omar and his wife without any shadow of doubt are not on an exploratory mission. Their sole mission is to go through the desert and enter Libya to continue their quest of crossing the Mediterranean and into Europe. They miss out on the Saharan landscapes as that is of no importance to them at all. An evening around a camp fire is not even remotely close to anything they want to do at this point of their journey. None of them is interested in sight seeing; the anxiety and the mission at hand will not allow any deviation from the plan at hand.

Omar and his wife were fortunate that their land cruiser was able to get through without encountering any rebels. "Crossing the desert was a long and difficult journey", Omar states. This was a journey that took hours under the hot sun and water, a necessity for survival did not come by easily. Omar explained that despite having little money, they never considered abandoning the journey. "You prefer to enter Europe and die there than go back", he said. He stated that after all the time, money and energy spent, they had to go on. There was just no turning back. He mentioned how the journey through the desert was so long. The distance from Agadez, to Al Qatrun, Libya is about 1600 miles. Depending on the transport you use, it can take twenty days or more. It took Omar and his wife about 4 days. They eventually arrived in Al Qatrun on the evening of August 25th 2013.

Upon arrival in Al Qatrun, Omar and Mary knew they were getting close to completing their mission but were not naive to that fact that they still had a long way to go.

In late September 2013, 92 people died of thirst attempting to cross the Sahara. This led to the government of Niger's move to shut down its decades-old desert migrant routes.

"We cannot remain indifferent in the face of this tragedy," Colonel Garba Maikido, the governor of the country's main northern town of Agadez told national radio. "We must take measures so that this type of tragedy never happens again on our territory."

Police raided dozens of transit houses, where would-be emigrants stay until heading off across the desert for North Africa and Europe beyond, and arrested a handful of smugglers and officials. About 50 policemen in the region around Agadez were replaced. Niger's government says large-scale migrant smuggling, which in effect was officially tolerated for years, has now ended.

But interviews with migrants, smugglers and officials in Agadez and in the capital Niamey tell a different story. The crackdown initially stemmed the flow of migrants. But the people smugglers have opened up new, more dangerous routes, and begun charging people more than ever to make the journey. The crackdown has ended the spectacular mass departures of the past, but migrants are still leaving the ancient trading town, often in small groups at night to meet up with 4x4s waiting in the desert. At least 13 migrants died in January 2014 after being abandoned by smugglers near the Niger-Algeria border, officials in northern Niger said.

The measures have also pushed the multi-million dollar business further into the hands of smuggling gangs, dominated by the Sahara's nomadic Toubou tribe.

The speed with which the trade has sprung back into life shows how hard it is for nations such as Niger to stop illegal emigrants from leaving. Often, the very people meant to police the immigrant routes are involved in the business themselves, say migrants, diplomats and an internal government report. So far, no one in a senior position has been charged with involvement in the trade.

Immigration has re-emerged as a hot topic in Europe as the continent recovers from years of economic hardship. Fringe parties are likely to score strongly in elections for the EU parliament later this month. Many demanding that borders be shut to new migrants or numbers be strictly rationed. But if trends in Agadez are anything to go by, the flow of migrants to Europe from West Africa is set to continue.

Although home to some of the continent's fastest growing economies, West Africa is struggling to generate enough jobs for its mushrooming young population. As a result, migrants from countries as diverse as oil-rich and democratic Ghana to The Gambia are still taking their chances by heading north to Europe, often through Agadez.

Trade took off in the mid-1990s, when countries like Spain and Italy imposed stricter visa requirements. Africans began making the dash across the Strait of Gibraltar, slipped into Spain's North African enclaves of Ceuta and Melilla, or attempted treacherous boat trips to the Canary Islands in the Atlantic or the Italian island of Lampedusa in the Mediterranean.

The popularity of routes changes as authorities adapt. A crackdown by Spanish and African authorities on the Canary Island route over recent years has meant more traffic through the Sahara. The violence and chaos of post-Gaddafi Libya has made things easier as well.

Given the nature of the trade, statistics on the numbers of those who try to cross the Sahara are sketchy. So many people die along the route and are not accounted for because their bodies get buried in the desert.

At least 34,800 people have made the treacherous crossing from North Africa to Europe in the first five months of 2014 as compared to 43,000 in all of 2013, according to figures from the U.N. refugee agency, UNHCR.

For years, the Agadez route operated largely in the open. Most people left in trucks and benefited from weekly escorts provided by Niger's military.

That changed with 2013's deaths. Most of the 92 were women and children who had been abandoned in the desert when the trucks they were in broke down. Marou Amadou, Niger's justice minister and the official government spokesman, said the incident galvanized public opinion and helped end a culture of denial.

"Nothing has changed," said Bachir Amadou, who works as a guide for Ghanaians headed for Libya. Amadou collects passports and cash from his eight charges for the next trip. Briefing them on what to expect, he tells them that on top of the 17,000 CFA ($36 or D1400) bus ticket, they will have to pay 43,000 CFA ($91 or D3540) in bribes to get through the police checkpoints between the capital and Agadez. For anyone without correct documents it will be double, he says.

Aboubacar Issaka Oumarou, Agadez's new police commissioner, said migrants were being ferried out at night to waiting Toyota Hilux pick-ups. Vehicles, often packed with 25-30 migrants at a time, have carved out fresh tracks through the desert to skirt around towns like Agadez.

"This puts the lives of the migrants in even more danger. But they (the smugglers) are not worried about this," Police Commissioner Oumarou said.

The fresh tracks are usually tracks that have not been travelled before thereby increasing the risk of being lost and potentially dying in the desert.

The Agadez-to-Libya route generated millions of dollars a year before the crackdown.

In Libya, smugglers await to snatch the money of any "Back Wayer" that has the funds to pay to be put on an easily capsized boat to be sent into the Mediterranean. In Libya, "Back Wayers" that do not have the funds wait for money from relatives back home so that they can pay to be smuggled. Some spend a few weeks, whereas others stay for months, before they can embark on the next leg of the journey. While in Libya, some seek work but many, may also end up in jails, for not only being in the country illegally, but also gaining illegal employment. Again, as in most legs of the journey, money gets you out of any situation. Usually, relatives back home are asked to foot the bill to get the "Back Wayers" out of any predicament they find themselves in.

Omar explained that he knew of few people that were kidnapped by someone they trusted to be a smuggler. The smuggler was to transport them to where the boats would be. However, they ended up at an unknown location. The man made it very clear that this was a kidnapping and provided a phone for them to call their families back home for ransom money. "They were so scared but were determined to make it", Omar said. Fortunately, this storyhad a good ending which is not always the case. Relatives were able to collect the funds and upon disbursement, the kidnappers set them free.

One of the most common routes by boat is from Libya to Italy. This is a longer and more unsafe route. Survivors often report violence and abuse by the smugglers who charge from a few hundred dollars to several thousands per person for their services.

Omar struggled to find work in Al Qatrun so he and his wife continued north to the city of Sabha.

Again the couple stayed put to earn money before taking the onward journey to Tripoli in November 2013. By then, Omar had been on the road for more than a year.

CHAPTER 7

Libya is a country in the Maghreb region of North Africa. It is bordered by The Mediterranean Sea to the north, Egypt to the east, Sudan to the southeast, Chad and Niger to the south and Algeria and Tunisia to the West. The three traditional parts of the country are Tripolitania, Fezzan and Cyrenaica. With an area of almost 1.8million square kilometers, Libya is the fourth largest country in Africa and the 18th largest in the world. Libya has the 10th largest proven oil reserves of any country in the world.

The largest city and capital, Tripoli is located in western Libya and contains over one million of Libya's six million people. The other large city is Benghazi, which is located in eastern Libya.

Muammar Gaddafi's reign ended when a civil war erupted in 2011, in which the rebels were supported by NATO. Since then, Libya has experienced instability and political violence which has severely affected both commerce and oil production. The European Union is involved in an operation to disrupt human smuggling networks fleeing the war for Europe. It is widely believed that the chaos in Libya is partly responsible or made it easier for the mass exodus of African Migrants trying to enter Europe.

Omar described life in Tripoli as "very tough". Despite finding work repairing phones, he was arrested for being an illegal immigrant.

In Libya it was all about the smuggling, a system that is not new. He stated that one gets by in Tripoli by word of mouth. Omar's plan was to make it to Libya, where he would stay and work to save money for him and his wife to continue the journey across the Mediterranean. He saw Tripoli as a very dangerous place and not a city he wanted to stay in. He knew they had to leave just as soon as they could.

He explained that the smugglers get you as far as Tripoli and that there are several places to pass through before making it to Tripoli. "The smugglers take care of you, because you need to be kept safe. You depend on them for all sorts of things", he said. The smugglers get you from point A to B. At point B, there are other smugglers who will get you to point C.

"Once you're in Tripoli, they [the smugglers] can keep you there if they want. They keep you in these special, fenced places. Innocent people are kept there for days or weeks because they're sick, or they don't have the money. Some end up being arrested. Some of them are kept for as long as two months, three months, because they can't contact their people. Some die there because of this. They call you when it's time to leave. You'll be there waiting then they [smugglers] call you. People get robbed. In Tripoli, I saw so many guns in the streets. You move, they shoot. They play with guns, they can steal your money. If you say you have no money on you, if they don't believe you, they wound people-unnecessarily. It's another crazy thing people face in Libya", explained Omar.

While Omar was in custody, his wife lost their first child, who died at birth.

> "She was too afraid to go to hospital for fear of being arrested and had to bury the baby with help from friends we'd made in Tripoli. I never saw my baby and I don't know where she was buried", Omar said.

Omar's wife borrowed money from friends to bail her husband out of prison and he returned to work in a mobile phone shop. It was there, through Libyan contacts that the couple learnt of a smuggler who took people to Italy for 800 Dinar each ($570 or D22800). Omar worked for several months in return for the crossing fare.

Then, one evening, the couple was driven to a beach not far from Tripoli to take the trip. The couple's boat left Libya at about 04:30 local time and by 14:00 they had reached international waters. The boat was made out of plastic and inflatable. It is spread, pumped and plywood applied at the bottom with some screws. This rubber dinghy can hold up to 80 people according to Omar's estimate.

> "There were about 100 people waiting, mainly from Nigeria, Senegal and The Gambia. The traffickers don't like to mix nationalities on the boats and keep people of similar language groups together. Nigerians, Malians, Gambians and

Senegalese would travel in one group. Somalians, Ethiopians and Eritreans in another and Syrians, Palestinians and other Arabs in another boat.

While at sea we had passed three or four capsized boats and there were clothes, food and other things floating on the water", said Omar.

Omar went on to explain how they saw a boat at sea that had already deflated and water was entering the boat. They saw several other boats with men, women and children. They left on a Friday night with no food or water from the smugglers. Most of the migrants on the boat were from Senegal, Mali and Nigeria.

On May 3rd 2015, a baby girl was born after her mother went into labor while being rescued from a boat in the Mediterranean. The baby was named Francesca Marina as a tribute to the Italian Navy. The Italian Navy crew found the Nigerian woman in labor in one of thirty four vessels intercepted the weekend of May 3rd.

After Omar and the rest of the migrants had been at sea all night, they made contact with the Italians around 2pm the next day. They however, were not rescued until nine hours later. He explained how the smugglers provide satellite phones or radios so they (the migrants) can contact the Italian coast guard as they approach the Italian coast.

Omar explained that there were so many boats in the sea that same night. They saw helicopters rescuing people from other boats but no help came to his boat.

> "Our boat was small and leaking so a group of
> men had to constantly use buckets to get rid of
> the water and keep us afloat," says Omar.

Eventually, a container ship arrived providing the smaller vessel with supplies. The crew threw down ropes to prevent the boat sinking until the Italian coastguards arrived to complete the rescue. The next morning they were taken off the rescue boat and put on another boat that took them to Sicily, Italy. He explained how elated he was as he knew their boat would have sunk had they spent another night on the waters as it was both overloaded and had already spent too much time on the water.

Once they were rescued, much needed food and water was given to them. Medical attention was also given to those that needed it.

Now, safely on Italian soil, Omar and his wife knew they were lucky to have survived their journey.

CHAPTER 8

The summer is usually the peak season for migrants arriving in Sicily. This is the end of the treacherous journey and is dubbed the 'boating' season. Awaiting officials are at the Sicilian port of Trapani; The officials range from nurses, doctors, coastguards, Police and Immigration officers.

Omar and Mary, part of a small group of five, approached the officials and things happened rapidly. They each wore a wristband and a surgical mask. After the wrist band and surgical masks were attached, a torch was used to view their ears and eyes and the routine continued on to the next migrants. This process continued until all those rescued were accounted for; a very tedious and time consuming process.

Several ships land in Italy but unfortunately, some of the boats capsize before being rescued. There were so many bodies that Italian officials have run out of place in the morgue refrigerators to store them. In October 2013, the Italian government created a naval rescue system called the Mare Nostrum. This was primarily due to the October 3rd incident where 366 Eritreans died when their boat sunk close to the shore of Lampedusa. During the Mare Nostrum operation, over 150,000 migrants, mainly from Africa and the Middle East, were rescued and arrived safely in Italy. Operation Mare Nostrum was a 9 million Euros per month bill to the Italian Government. It lasted for 12 months and became too much for one nation to handle. On November 1st 2014, it was replaced by operation Triton, an EU initiative which was conducted by

Frontex, the European Union's border security union. This operation is under Italian control, but involves voluntary contributors from 15 other European nations. The two operations however, were meant to be complimentary, not alternatives to each other. The Mare Nostrum cost European citizens over 114million euros annually, whereas the Triton only costs 35million euros annually. The mission to rescue at sea has now been reduced to the EU's stated primary objective in terms of migration; protecting the borders.

Omar and Mary, after having been at sea for four to five days, were naturally in awe and rarely said much, all the while wondering what's going to happen next. Several Italian volunteers were on deck to hand out shoes and provide food to these migrants as they awaited the next phase. The IOM also has representatives at the ports of entry.

Until 2011, ships leaving Libya and entering Italy were turned back whenever possible. That is no longer the case for the government of Matteo Renzi has raised a humanitarian flag and has been quoted as saying that saving lives is their top priority. Italian Police and immigration officers are next in line for the rescued migrants to go through.

Omar and Mary knew that where they would end up, depended upon their interview with the immigration officials. They planned on concocting a story about how they feared persecution if they got returned to their homelands. Based on information they had gathered from those that attempted the journey, this story could possibly give them an asylum.

The Dublin regulation is an EU law stating that asylum applications must be handled by the first EU country they entered. Most of these migrants would rather seek asylum in another EU country than Italy. However, according to the Dublin regulation, they are not allowed to apply for asylum in another European destination outside of Italy. There are exceptions though, including some meant to unite or reunite with their families.

The "Dublin Regulation" and the "Schengen" are two policies that loom large in the migrant crisis. The former is an EU law that determines which nation is responsible for processing the requests of asylum seekers from outside the union. The latter is an agreement to abolish border controls among European nations that have joined. Due to the 'Dublin regulation", Italy is swamped with migrants resulting in European leaders arguing on how to distribute the burden more evenly across Europe. The Schengen depends on each member nation trusting the others to control who enters the Schengen area from outside. The recent flood of migrants however, has overwhelmed those controls in some countries.

All those over the age of 18 without a work permit, family connection or history of political persecution, are termed "irregular migrants". They are usually held in detention camps until an expulsion order comes through. A refugee status (Asylum) is granted only to those who can prove they risked persecution or death in their country of origin. If immigration officials believe a migrant's asylum claim is genuine, they are placed in a SPRAR (Protection System for Asylum and Refugees). If there's no space in the SPRAR, the migrant will be placed in a CARA (Accommodation Center for Asylum seekers), until their case goes before commission.

Fortunately for Omar and his wife, the immigration officials believed their asylum case was genuine. They were given a number on a piece of paper and were then taken to the CARA (Accommodation Center for Asylum seekers), where they awaited their asylum case.

The very next morning, when they had access to a telephone, they called their families back in The Gambia and Burkina Faso. Their families were elated to hear from them.

The CARA di Mineo is one of Italy's largest asylum-seeker reception centres. Official capacity is set at 2,000 but behind its fence, way more than that number of occupants inhabit its block of apartments at any given time.

By law, Asylum-seekers can only be held for 35 days in a CARA. In reality, the average stay is closer to a year. The Italian state pays the organization 34.60 Euros per day, per immigrant, in rent, which averages close to 50 million euros annually. While at the CARA, migrants are allowed to leave and come as they wish but they are supposed to clock back in every evening. For those that want to be out overnight, permission must be sought ahead of time. The remote location of the CARA, along with limited resources, makes most of the asylum seekers not leave at all.

CARA di Mineo is an apartment housing surrounded by barbed wire and armed guard. The CARA is completely out of place in the rural Sicilian landscape that surrounds it. Planted in the middle of nowhere, the center has been described as "una cattedrale nel deserto" – a cathedral in the desert, which is another way of calling it a white elephant.

The grounds were originally used by the personnel of a US military air station. The facility includes a sports ground, as well as a bar and play area for children. In September 2015, the vast complex sheltered just over 3,000 asylum seekers, down from nearly 4,000 in the past but critics demanding its closure feel the number is still too high.

> "Mineo is a town of 5,000 people, but many of them are elderly and there are few youngsters. So the arrival of colored migrants, all of them young, who hang around doing nothing, often make the townsfolk afraid", said Mayor Aloisi, a member of Italy's new Centre Right Party.

In the CARA, the migrants are divided by ethnicity and religion and reside in 403 yellow and pink houses, sleeping several to a room on foam mattresses, eating in the cafeteria or cooking over small stoves in their back gardens.

> "There's talk of prostitution, of drug trafficking, there is certainly a lively black market.
>
> The residents sell clothes, food, cigarettes and phone cards at bazaars dotted around the center, there's even an illicit restaurant and a migrant-run taxi service. These controls are far and few in between," said Angela Lupo, a legal adviser for the Italian Council for refugees (CIR)

Omar, along with the other asylum seekers at the CARA di Mineo felt confined and frustrated by the long delays, overcrowding, isolation and because they had little or nothing to do.

In September 2015, it was revealed that organized crime groups had infiltrated the centre's management. This left the government red-faced and Minister Maria Elena Boschi promised parliament that the camp was under review and closure was an option.

As the crisis intensified across Europe, on September 4th 2015, Pope Francis called for Christian parishes to take in refugees; A sentiment applauded by those in favor of doing away with unwieldy centres, as well as the migrants themselves.

An outcry in a country tired of being on the frontline of Europe's largest refugee crisis since World War II, was sparked by the September 2015 grisly murder of a local couple that led to a subsequent arrest of an Ivorian man from the Sicilian center.

For Omar, Mary and anyone staying at CARA di Mineo, integration is nothing short of a physical impossibility. The centre is simply a massive waiting room for the residents hoping to get the documents that will allow them to start their new lives as soon as possible.

According to the CIR, many residents see little of the services which state funding should ensure. These services included Italian lessons, legal help and medical care and can only play football while waiting for their paperwork to be handled, which can take up to two years.

Omar and his wife patiently waited at the CARA for the next steps of their case. They received Legal aid offered by some NGOs (Non-Governmental Organizations) such as the IOM, to help them prepare.

While at the CARA, they met several other Africans. Among the Africans was a 21 year old Gambian, named Kebba, who had also made it to Italy via the "Back Way". He, like all the other people at the CARA had stories to tell.

Omar asked him why he decided to embark on this journey and how he ended up at the CARA.

> "My mother who I love so much was struggling to take care of us and was not okay. Nothing seemed to be working out for us. So I had no choice but to embark on this journey," answered Kebba.

This is a very common story among most "Back Wayers" so it's clear that economic problems, and not political persecution, are the main reasons why so many take on this brutal and often fatal journey.

Kebba explained that he had tried other ways and means of traveling and gaining employment in The Gambia but nothing seemed to materialize.

Kebba went on to explain how his mother helped him raise the funds required to start the journey. Omar explained that he could sense Kebba's reluctance to talk about what his mother had to go through to secure the funds. Omar understood the feeling just too well. He remembered how reluctant his parents were to let him go but could not admonish him.

Kebba went on to explain how almost all of his mother's relatives vehemently expressed concerns over this journey and how they were totally against it.

> "I did not care what anyone said, I had to go" he
> said somberly.

After securing enough funds to leave The Gambia, Kebba went ahead and also had his ID card duplicated with up to 20 copies. He left The Gambia in the middle of the night on a bus along with several other "Back Wayers". This bus was supposed to take them all the way to Agadez, Niger, where he would proceed to Libya and then to Italy across the Mediterranean. He explained how he thought he had paid for a trip that would take him all the way to Agadez. However, upon arrival in Mali, he was informed by the driver that they had reached the final destination. Evidently he had been duped. He resorted to calling his mother to explain what had transpired. She obviously, was in a panic but he promptly assured her that he still had money to hop on a bus that would get him into Agadez. Several other migrants were in the same predicament as him but they were able to figure their way out of Mali into Agadez. The journey through the desert was such a long one. He explained how he had nothing to do but simply sit on the bus with anxiety. Several checkpoints had to be gone through and at each one he had to pay up just like all others aboard.

Again, a very familiar sentiment to Omar. He and his wife had to pay their entire way. A bribe got them out of any predicament they found themselves in.

Kebba spent several days going through the desert and it was a big sigh of relief when they finally reached Agadez. "Smuggler information is provided right on the bus" he recalled.

From Agadez, he was whisked along with several other migrants in the back of a pickup truck into Tripoli. A journey that seemed like it would never end. A journey through the desert where they saw so many dead and rotted bodies. A four day journey.

"Tripoli was a mess and brutal to black Africans. These people do not care for anyone who is not from Libya. They do care for our money though and they all think we have money", he said.

He explained how even though he did not experience any kidnapping, he knew of a lot of migrants that experienced it and had to phone back home to get ransom money.

When they arrived in Tripoli, there were smuggler agents telling them who to go with and why one smuggler was better than the other. The boat trip into Italy cost about $800 (D32000) and he knew he did not have that kind of money. He called his mother who, as expected, did not have the funds either. She told him to stay put while she sorted things out. He waited for 3 long weeks in Tripoli until his mother could come up with the money. While in Tripoli he laid low because he was in fear of being mugged or even jailed. At no point did he contemplate abandoning the journey.

> "No waaay". I did not want to come across as a failure. Of course you hear stories about boats capsizing and many migrants drowning but Europe is all about luck. I had to go on", said Kebba.

This is a very familiar sentiment and one harboured by most that undertake this perilous journey. The reality however, is that "Europe is not all about luck". Unlike Omar, Kebba had been unable to secure work in Libya. Actually, it was not even in his plans. The money from his mother finally arrived, three weeks later, via western union. He counted the money and it was enough to get him into Italy on a dinghy across the Mediterranean. He had already made 'smuggler' contacts and all he'd been waiting on was the funds. On that same day, he contacted his smuggler to find out when the next boat was departing. He was informed of a boat that was leaving the next day. He disbursed the funds to the smuggler and was told that someone will pick him up to take him to the boat for departure.

According to Kebba, the owner of the boat does not embark on the crossing of the Mediterranean. The "captain" of the boat himself is a "Back Wayer" and due to his services, he does not pay for the journey.

He is given a compass, a Walkie-talkie and given a crash course on how to navigate the boat and when to radio for help.

> "We left in the middle of the night and were not rescued until the early hours of the morning," he said. All 150 of us on board were so scared at times. You can hear folks arguing with the "captain" who they accused of not knowing how to navigate", he explained.

He explained to Omar that although he was scared, he just maintained his cool and uttered a lot of prayers. Per the instructions provided by the smugglers, the "captain" used the walkie-talkie to radio for help from the Italian coast guard once they approached the Italian coast. Once contact with Italian Coast Guard was made, he [the captain] discarded the compass and the walkie-talkie as he was instructed. To avoid a trace back of the walkie-talkie to them, the smugglers made it clear to the captain that he had to discard both the compass and the walkie-talkie. Once contact is made with the Italian officials, they asked them who was onboard. Were there any women and children?

The reason for these questions was to prioritize the rescue missions, as there were so many of them to handle in a given night.

Once they were rescued, they were on the sea for another 4 days before reaching Sicily. He explained that it was on the rescue ship that they were processed. They were fingerprinted and interviewed by immigration. They were well fed he recalled, food they clearly needed. The authorities did a health check on each and every one of them. In

Italy, after completion of all immigration paper work and pending asylum, they were taken to a camp referred to as the "campus" by migrants.

> "This campus is CARA di Mineo and that is how I ended up here" Kebba told Omar.

Kebba explained to Omar that the asylum process takes up to a year in some cases and all one can do is wait. He told Omar that he had been at the CARA for 5 months at that time. A few that had been there with him were less patient and found ways to get out of Italy and into Germany or neighboring countries.

Kebba said that for any single, young man trying to tackle the journey, he would encourage him but for a family man, he would tell him not do it. He then looked at Omar and asked if that was his wife next to him. To which, Omar answered in the affirmative.

> "Brother, you are a soldier. Tackling this journey with a wife is a huge task and I commend you", Kebba said to Omar.

In Italy, Omar and Mary got help to complete their asylum papers from several non-governmental organizations. Even though Asylum seekers are supposed to be at the CARA for no more than thirty five days, Omar and Mary were there for ten months before being granted protection. While at the CARA, they both took courses in Italian to prepare for integration into Italian society.

Once they were granted protection in Italy, they left the CARA and moved on to the SPRAR. This is a system of reception and integration run by the Ministry for Internal Affairs. It is in collaboration with humanitarian organisations, to offer asylum seekers and refugees accommodation and help to integrate into Italian society.

Ideally, accommodating a few residents each, SPRAR centres are usually located in the heart of cities and towns all over Italy. In June 2014, there were 19,000 places available. In August, the emergency parallel system set up by the Italian government was accommodating an additional 25,000 people. However, demand still falls far short of need. So even if technically speaking, refugees have the right to live in a SPRAR centre or other accommodation, many can still end up with nowhere to go.

In Catania, some find temporary shelter in five dormitories run by NGOs and the Missionaries of Charity, as well as a few other places including the city mosque. But countless people sleep on the streets; Recognised refugees together with others awaiting the outcome of the appeal on their rejected asylum application and still, others who evaded the system altogether. They sleep at bus stops, at the train station, on patches of grass and benches, in abandoned cars and under stone arcades.

Sometimes they are chased away. Some find a place in abandoned factories or warehouses by the harbour.

After thirteen months, Omar and Mary finally got asylum and they both secured work at a restaurant.

> "I am determined to work as a mobile phone technician in Europe and support my wife as well as my extended family in The Gambia. The Gambia is very different from Italy. In The Gambia, you would never be allowed to spend the night outside. Strangers are appreciated in The Gambia. I never imagined that in Italy people would be hungry and spend nights outside as I have seen on numerous occasions", said Omar.

Omar and his wife started a Facebook group to explain the dangerous nature of this perilous journey. Instead of people heeding their advice, they were flooded with messages from potential "Back Wayers" in need of smuggler information.

CHAPTER 9

From Omar's story, we know that being stranded in Mali or any of the cities along this treacherous route could pose serious issues as the country has little to offer the "Back Wayer". We can also conclude that the pay is very meagre and in some cases, could take months to gather enough money to continue the route. In fact, a very safe conclusion is that being stranded in any of these African countries could have very serious consequences. The "Back Wayer" who is now an illegal immigrant has to tread along very fine lines as he continues to risk being arrested, deported, or even put in jail, especially if he has no money to bribe his way. Once he is able to somehow gather enough money to pay for smugglers or the like, the journey continues. It is very seldom that we read of a "Back Wayer" getting married along the way as was the case in Omar's story. We however have read about husbands and wives as well as an entire family embarking on this journey.

On most of the buses that terminate in Agadez, smuggler information is provided right on the bus. The entire journey is really about the smugglers; getting the right smuggler to put you on to the next phase of your journey. This is something that has been in place for a very long time. You have to trust the smugglers to get you through and to keep you safe. However, it is the same smuggler to whom you entrust your life with that ends up, in some cases being responsible for its end.

Once the "Back Wayers" arrive in Libya, a major part of their journey has been accomplished. Libya as emphasized by all those interviewed is the worst phase of the journey. Yet it is the one country a "Back Wayer" cannot wait to arrive in.

Europe is not paved with gold as many of these "Back Wayers" quickly find out. Racism is just one of the few concerns and blending into society presents a huge challenge. Without the proper education and skills, many of these folks struggle to find gainful employment thusly having to resort to activities that may end up getting them deported or put in jail.

CHAPTER 10

On November 11, 2015, The European Union pressed African leaders to take back thousands of people who do not qualify for asylum. According to the IOM, almost 800,000 people have entered Europe by sea in 2015; A number that could be more than 3 million by 2017.

To further demonstrate the dangerous route and problems faced in Libya as well as the main reasons why these people embark on this journey, below are personal accounts of different African Migrants that took on the journey. One statement that sums it all up for most readers is, "If I knew more about the journey, I would never have come." Undoubtedly, this is a common sentiment harbored by the majority of those that took on such a daunting endeavor.

Samuel, 24, Ivory Coast

"There was too much violence in Ivory Coast. You can't live there. All my friends had left. My parents divorced and didn't look after me. I was nine when I had to drop out of school. I started working to look after myself and put some money aside, little by little. I went to Libya. I worked as an upholsterer so I could pay my rent and buy food. But at the end of the day, they would stop me in the street and take my money. I lived on eggs: they were cheap. But that wasn't the problem. After almost two years, it became too violent and dangerous.

Libyans don't like anyone who is not Libyan. I was feeling bad; I had no choice but to leave again.

I looked for someone who could help me. I asked around, paid lots of money, and in three days I left. It was at night. There were more than 500 of us on that boat. Far too many. I didn't see anything when I boarded, it was dark; but once I was inside, I immediately thought, I'm going to die. Two hours into the journey, the engine broke. I thought, it's over now. The sea, you know, it's not just a bit of water. I was ready for the end.

After two days, they rescued us. They gave us food – macaroni. I hadn't eaten in two days, so it was good. You must go to a country where there is security and where human rights are respected, even if the risk is dying in the water".

Ibrahim, 29, and Sidibe, 10, Mali

Ibrahim: I was born in Congo-Brazzaville. My father died in the Congo war and I moved to Mali with my mother. My brother Sidibe was born to another dad. One day, on television, I saw people who had made it to Italy. I was working in Congo-Brazzaville and decided to go there via Libya. I stopped in Mali, and during my stay my mother died. My brother was left alone, so I took him with me. But the journey was long and once we arrived in Libya, it was terrible.

Sidibe: It was a very long journey. We travelled by bus from Algeria to Libya. The dust was so much – I really suffered. Then I had to walk for three hours across the border. I was tired. When we arrived in Ghadames, on the Libyan border, they gave me bread and cheese. That was so nice. Then they put us on a truck and I had to sit on sheep's poo. I threw up. Later, we found a house. One night, at midnight, some policemen knocked at our door and took my brother away. I stayed alone at home for four days. I didn't know what to do. I had only biscuits and water. I was frightened and thought I was not going to see Ibrahim again. I only have him.

Ibrahim: I had done nothing, but they were armed and took me to prison. They said nothing, only asked for lots of money – 500,000 West African CFA francs ($770 or D31000) – if I wanted to be freed. Once I was out, I started putting money aside for the journey by boat. On the night we departed, I saw lots of people dying around me. To get on board, you need to walk from the shore into the sea until the water reaches your shoulders. Then you are pushed on the dinghy. It's there that people fall and die. The boat was crowded. I jumped on it and put Sidibe between my legs. We spent three days like this. The sea was going up and down, we were taking on water. When the rescue ship arrived, Sidibe was pulled to safety first. The Italians gave us food and water. They are good people. Now I want Sidibe to go to school.

Promise, 26, Nigeria.

There was plenty of war in Nigeria. I lost my mother and father, my sisters and my brothers – we all ran away during the war, and I don't know where they are now.

A man saved me from the war and took me to his house, but his wife thought I was sleeping with him. He gave me some money and told me to flee to Libya. But when I got there, I saw there was war, too. I found myself in Tripoli. There was fighting and killing all around us. Libya is a Muslim country; they don't like Christians like me.

Somebody brought me to his house and told me to stay. They said they would help me go to Italy. But that house wasn't a good one. It was very big and there were other people. I stayed for a long time, I can't remember how long. Then somebody paid for me to get on a boat and come here. The journey was very long. I thought I was going to die. The sea was very big and dark. I was crying inside that boat: God help me, God save me. I prayed with another woman – we didn't know each other. Finally we saw a ship coming. It was in the afternoon. We thought they were fishermen, but it was a rescue boat. We were waving, crying, shouting: help, help! And so [the Italians] came and rescued us. A man from the ship grabbed my hand – "don't rush, don't rush", he said. I still remember him-he was slim and had a cap on his head. Thank God, I said. I'm happy now, but I feel very alone.

Maryan, Somalia

"My dad went to Canada when I was born. A year later, I moved with my mum to Kenya; there was fighting in Somalia. I have a sister and four brothers. We stayed in a UNHCR refugee camp. That's where I learned English; I studied there. We wanted to get visas for America, but we are Africans, you know? They sent us back to Somalia instead.

One day, a few years ago, al-Shabab brought our house down. There was an explosion. My mother died; I still miss her. I have a husband back home and two children. They live in a town between Somalia and Ethiopia.

I didn't tell anyone that I wanted to leave, initially – only a friend. She helped me organize my travel to Libya, then to Italy, to go to America. I want to give my family a good life. While moving countries and phone numbers, we lost contact with my dad. But I want to find him now. I have an aunt, his sister, in the US. That's where I want to go".

Faith, 25, Nigeria

"My mother died when she gave birth to me. I was four when I also lost my dad. I was staying with my grandma – no school, nothing – but six years ago, she died as well. I went to stay with one of my aunties in Kano, northern Nigeria, but there was fighting all over. Boko Haram (an Islamic extremist group based in northeastern Nigeria) was there, so I came back home.

One of my friends said she was going to Libya, so I followed her in December last year. When we reached Sabha [a hub of the trafficking trade in the south-west], I was kidnapped together with another woman. They kept us in a room with five more women. No food to eat, nothing for four days. Until, one night, a man we didn't know helped us escape. He told us to run, that the place was not safe for us.

It was night-time. We ended up by the sea. The man said we should get on a boat – there were lots of people. The next day, around two in the afternoon, they came to rescue us. I'm OK now, but every time I think of my past, I stop eating. People call their mum and dad. I didn't know my mum. I have no one to call".

Samba, 30, The Gambia

"I came to find a better future in Europe. Because of poverty in our country – in all African countries. This makes people run away.

I come from a very extended family. My father is not alive, there are 17 of us, and they all rely on me. I'm a mobile technician – I repair phones. Out of the little money I was earning, three-quarters went to the family. It was not enough to satisfy me, let alone them. I heard you could make a lot of money in Libya. All my friends in The Gambia left to go there.

They told me that the province was safe, that you can work and earn money. I stayed almost three years, but then the problems spread across the country. They kidnapped blacks everywhere, demanding £1,200-£2,000 as a ransom. After a year, my brother joined me in Libya, but he was injured at work and died. There was no hospital to take him to. It was too dangerous.

They kidnap you in the street, but it's better to be taken by the bandits than the police; at least the kidnappers want to keep you alive to get the money from your family.

I was put in prison, and given very little food. My family didn't have any money to pay. Once I was out, I started working, but didn't get paid. Then I was offered a chance to come to Italy. The people who do this don't hide; they approach you in the street. Even the police approach people. My boat was a dinghy. We were more than 100 people, and my family knew nothing about it. Nobody on the boat expected such a bad journey, but it would have been better to die in the water on the way to Italy than to stay in Libya. One day, I will go back home".

Kwame, 25, Ghana

"I didn't want to come to Europe. I wanted to work in Libya. I stayed there for two years. But then I thought I was going to die, so I decided to leave. But from Libya you can't get a car or jump on a plane. If you try to cross the border, you will be shot.

I took a boat to Italy because it's near. If I knew more about the journey, I would never have come. They pushed us on the boat; there were 93 of us, fighting for our lives in that tiny boat. We didn't know if the captain was qualified. I cried. The boat began to sink and the captain called the rescue ship. It was eight o'clock when it arrived.

They took me to a reception center. There were 400 of us at the beginning. Now they have moved 300 people, taking them to Rome and Milan. I don't have anything with me here. I don't have my family's phone numbers. All I had was a memory card that they stole from me before I jumped on the boat. We've been sitting here for two weeks now. We spend the day walking up and down. You don't know what is going on. I want to work. My family in Ghana has nothing. I am hopeful that something will change".

Valerie, 27, Ivory Coast

"This dress is the only thing I have with me. It's old, but it's my favorite and reminds me of my three girlfriends back home. I bought it for New Year's Eve. We had fun that night, watching the fireworks. I washed it after the journey by boat. It was soaked.

I left Ivory Coast because my parents were planning a forced marriage. I'm a Muslim, and I refused. My father kicked me out. I decided to join my brother in Tripoli. I travelled across Burkina Faso and via Agadez in Niger [part of a well-known traffickers' route], then through Libya.

Every time you come into contact with the "police", you have to pay. I spent a week in Sabha, where we paid people to take us to Tripoli. There, we were sold again to different people, who then sold us on.

When they take you, they make you work. In Libya I was kidnapped and put in prison for a month. I was raped many times. There were lots of women like me. I was sharing a cell with a girl from Mali and one from Nigeria. We communicated with our hands, and the Nigerian girl became a friend.

Our dream was to come to Europe. My brother paid £218 to help me – his friends had raised some money to free me. But then I became ill – I couldn't eat, I couldn't sleep. I was worried the people from the prison would come again. So he organized my travel to Europe. I've been here two weeks. I just want to work".

Joy, 20, Nigeria

I left Nigeria because of Boko Haram. They killed my parents, my sisters, my brothers. My friend and I didn't know where to go, we wanted to save our lives. A man took us to Libya, but he put us into prostitution. I had no food, and if I refused to do what he wanted, he would beat me and threaten me with a gun.

I was forced to work as a prostitute for a year. We managed to run away and met a man who paid for us to get on a boat. I was praying to my God. Now I'm here with my best friend. But I'm sad when I think about my family. I want to become a journalist, a newscaster. I will try my best".

Karim, 30, Mali

I'm here because of the war. In Mali, I was repairing motorbikes. One day I came home after work and found that my mother had been killed. My little sister had been killed. They were dead on the floor. I asked myself, why wasn't I there?

Then I thought, if I had been there, they would have killed me, too. I ran out and flew to Algeria. But once I arrived, I discovered that it was difficult to find a job and make a living. There are no motorbikes there, only cars. I became worried. I moved to Tripoli to be able to eat. There's more work, but it's also more dangerous.

In the street, if they see you're a foreigner, they will shout, "Come here!" If you don't run, they'll beat you. They hit me many times, once with the back of a gun. I found a job cleaning the houses of wealthy people. But on the way back from work, they would strip me of my clothing and take the money I had earned. Once, I went three days without eating. I had to look for food in the rubbish.

One day, a man offered to pay for me to go to Italy. There was war in Libya. Even that night – "boom boom" – you could hear it. I thought, I'll leave. That's why I'm here. But I still have so much sorrow. My life is finished without my mother and sister. There was a time when I wanted to get married and have a family, but now I don't. My children would ask me, "Where is grandma?" I loved my mother. I don't care about finding a woman.

Rose, 21, Nigeria

"I wanted to become a nurse in Nigeria, but when my family was murdered right in front of me, I decided to escape. I met a man and told him I needed help, since I was an orphan – no one to talk to, just me. He said he was going to take me to Libya to work in a restaurant with him. I went, not knowing that he was bringing me there to work as a prostitute and make money for him. He told me that when we arrived in Libya.

I said to him, "I can't do it." He locked me up for some months and beat me every night and day. There was nowhere to escape. There were lots of people like me in the same room. No one could hear us. Sometimes, they didn't even give us food.

One day, a man came to the house. I told him, "I can't continue staying in this place. Please help me." He said OK, on the condition that I follow him to his house. I went, not knowing he was taking me to the seaside. So, all of a sudden, I found myself on the Mediterranean Sea.

We were many; I was really scared. The water has no end and no beginning. A lot of people were fighting with sharp objects. There were Muslims and Christians. They said they didn't want Christians on the boat. I was one of them. Then the heat burned one of the girls. I cried. God, did this man bring me out of that place to kill me in the water? I can't even explain it. A lot of things happened before we saw the rescue ship. I was very happy then. Now I want the UN to help me. I don't want to sell myself for money".

Simon, 32, Nigeria.

"I came because I wanted some peace-that's why I ran away from Nigeria but I have found no peace. I was detained for a year in Malta. They don't care about you here. If somebody dies, they don't care they just put you in a grave and that's it. They don't try to find your family.

There's nothing good about life here. I feel like it's all upside down".

The names in the testimonials above have been changed.

Here are more testimonies of those that tackled the journey and successfully made it to Italy only to realize, it was not what they expected.

Karoli, 23, Ghana

"It's boring inside the camp, you have to queue for one or two hours to eat, sometimes fights break out in the line. You cannot really create space for 4,000 people to eat, can you? I never thought I would leave my country but when I had to do so, and I crossed the sea to Lampedusa, I thought I had come to a free life. But now I see it is not so. I know that if I have documents, I can continue my life, go to school, learn the language, and look for work."

Musa, 21, The Gambia

"I've been here at CARA di Mineo for nearly one year and three months. I received a negative decision and I am appealing because I know that if you are here without documents, you are nothing. This is why I am still here, sitting in one place, not doing anything, not going anywhere, because I am waiting. Here at CARA di Mineo, it's not like morning is easy and night is tough, it's always difficult. You have to queue for everything. Sometimes, getting meals is a problem. Because there are so many people, you have to stay in a queue for two hours to get food. I can't be in a queue every day for so many months. We want to leave this kind of life, to be free and to benefit the country that has helped us. We are still under control here, and it's very different from being on our own. I am definitely tired, this is a camp, not a city, it is really too much. I need documents. I've never experienced something like this before. I want to leave this system, to be free."

Pa Lamin, 25, The Gambia

"Before it was worse at CARA di Mineo. The way they were taking care of us was very bad, just food and that's all. We had to protest for clothes, toothpaste, soap, and then they would give you once and that's it. Something else is that the Italian teachers at CARA di Mineo could only speak Italian. It was difficult for us to understand and I was discouraged. I had a copybook where I used to write things in English and then I would go to people working at CARA to ask 'what is the meaning of this or that?' They would write in Italian and that's how I started picking up some words."

Solomon, 30, Burkina Faso

"We were rescued at sea and brought to Lampedusa. We stayed for three days before they brought us here to CARA di Mineo. The time to go before the commission is too long for us, 10, 11 months. They feed us and look after us here – we are ok. We can go to Italian classes if we want, we have a football field. We have advice, social workers, free healthcare. But what I want to see in this camp is job opportunities – we need to do something."

John, 30, Ghana

"When we came to CARA di Mineo and saw the military, we believed we would be shut up here, like in Libya, and we were afraid. I spent one year and two months in Mineo. There are many ethnic groups there and this always caused problems. The houses were overcrowded and even going to the bathroom posed a problem: you had to queue. To get clothes, again you had to queue. Also, we could not study Italian well because there were too many people in class, around 50 at times, and we could not understand what the teacher was saying. What I'll never forget is the time an Eritrean man killed himself because he got a negative response to his asylum application. This was very bad. We came here to have freedom, we didn't come here to find more problems, to be shut up in an isolated place where we don't know anything, because that place is too far away from Catania and anywhere else, practically in the bush."

Sophia, 24, Senegal

"I want to stay here at CARA di Mineo to be a cultural mediator because there isn't one for my country. At first, I wasn't happy here, but now it's ok. I have friends and also I am thinking of work – it would be good if I could get this job. The Italians who work here are good. Although life at CARA is ok, one problem is that now the houses are very crowded. Another thing is the clinic: they told my friend he would need 2,500 Euros for an operation in his nose, they did nothing to help him and he can't breathe or sleep well at night. We earn nothing here, how could he pay that money?"

Michael, 22, Ivory Coast

"I get very upset when I see the others here at CARA di Mineo calling their families back home because I don't have anyone to call. I stay inside my room all the time. I only go out to eat and I go back to my room. There is nowhere to go and I have no friends. Actually I can leave now because I have a paper to show I am appealing my asylum decision. But I am staying here because I have nobody, where can I go?"

The testimonies above are from individuals that had dealings with the CARA. From these testimonies, we gather that life in the CARA is definitely not what most expected it to be.

Below are testimonies from migrants that were assisted by Caritas. "Caritas Internationalis" is a confederation of Catholic relief, development and social service organizations operating in over 200 countries and territories worldwide.

Matthieu, 25, Ivory Coast

"When I came to Catania I spent a month sleeping outside. Then I stayed in a dormitory for nearly a year. We had to go in at 8pm and leave at 6am even if we had nowhere to go, even if we were sick, even if it was cold, we had to leave and stay outside. I didn't know what to do, there was nothing to do, just sitting and thinking, all the time."

Lamin, 22, The Gambia

"At first I was sleeping in the streets then Caritas found me a place to stay called Il Faro. I am happy there because I am not sleeping outside. To sleep in the street is not easy, all my bones used to hurt me. Even now, if I sleep in a bed, after two hours, I wake up in pain. I used to sleep on a carton, and that was all I had. I was alone. Sometimes I stayed at a bus stop, sometimes at the train station, placing my carton on the bench. I didn't even have blankets. Every day I went to eat at Caritas. I would go to the town and ask friends to give me one or two Euros to buy bread."

Kofi, 22, Ghana

"When we arrived in Catania, we went to Caritas but they told us they have no place – we were outside for months, sleeping on the streets. Then Caritas found a place for us. We don't do anything in the day because there is no work; this is very difficult for me. So I have started Italian school and later I walk around to see if I can find anything to do... I look for a place to sit down and wait until it is time to go back to the dormitory. What experiences will I never forget? The experience of sleeping outside in very cold weather, that was very bad, and of staying idle, without doing anything."

Godwin, 27, Afghanistan

"Norway was a good place to be. I was there for three years and I had a job, a place to live and food, but no documents. When they wanted to deport me, I worried about what would happen if they returned me to Afghanistan. So I came here because I heard Italy was good for refugees. But I spent two years without documents, without a home, without food or money. For three months I lived on the street without spare clothes or food. It was a bad time. In winter it was so cold, especially when it rained, and I was very sick. I wanted to die. I thought, why is this happening? One day, I thought about my family and country, and I felt so bad – it is so bad there and so bad here, how can I live? Then a friend helped me and took me to his place, I paid him when I could. I changed accommodation many times... one day one place and then another place the next because I had no money except when I found odd jobs here and there."

Abraham, 25, Eriteria

"When they give you a document at CARA, they take you to the train station and drop you off, without even one euro in your hand. You really don't know where to start. I left after a year and a half. I went to a SPRAR house near Agrigento, we were four residents, but I was not very happy there. There was nothing to do, I had no money in my pocket and I was learning nothing. So I left. I spent two years sleeping outside and it was difficult even to get food to eat. I tried going to Italy. I stayed in a place called the Ghetto outside Foggia in the south, a settlement where hundreds of African migrants live. Italian people go there to collect them for work. If you see this place and they tell you human beings live here, you won't believe it; it's terrible. 'Houses' are made out of carton, poles and rope. The ground is like clay and everything is dirty. I lost my documents there so I came back to Catania. It was very difficult to get them replaced, it has taken me over a year, and still it's not over. Back in Catania, I slept at the train station, in the rain in winter and the heat in summer. Actually we were outside because the station is closed at night. If we wanted to go inside because it was raining, the police would drive us away. There were many of us; we had nowhere to go. We used to go to Caritas to eat. It was a very bad experience, I felt like going out of this world because I had nothing to give me joy at that time. Not only did I have nothing, there was nothing I could do to get the things I needed, no one to give me the links to start somewhere. It was just faith that kept me going, I told myself, 'leave it in the hands of God, whatever God says, it is going to be like that.' Even if you go now to the train station, you will see women sleeping there with their children, from Eritrea, Somalia and other countries, it's not fair."

As with all the testimonies, the names have been changed to protect the identity of the narrators. The stories are very disheartening and some could simply bring tears to the reader's eyes.

CHAPTER 11

Based on the data compiled by IOM, the large majority of deaths in 2014 occurred in the Mediterranean. This accounted for an estimated 75 per cent (3,072) of all deaths that year. Therefore making it the deadliest sea in the world for migrants. Since 2000, numbers compiled over time, show at least 22,400 people are estimated to have lost their lives trying to reach Europe. This means on average nearly 1,500 migrants died each year during this period. Based on available data, 2014 represents the deadliest year in this time period. More than twice as many deaths occurred in the first nine months of that year than took place during the Arab Spring of 2011. An estimated 1,500 lost their lives crossing the Mediterranean (UNHCR, 2012). This figure is almost five times higher than the 630 migrants who are estimated to have died or gone missing in the Mediterranean in 2007, which is the peak number prior to 2011. Deaths in recent months have reached devastating levels, with the deadliest shipwreck claiming an estimated 500 lives in early September (IOM, 2014).

The reasons for these differences have not been fully investigated but the jump in the number of fatalities in the Mediterranean in 2014 likely reflects a dramatic increase in the number of migrants trying to reach Europe. In 2014 numbers spiked, over 112,000 arrivals by sea of irregular migrants as reported by the Italian authorities. Many are fleeing conflict, persecution and poverty. The Eritreans and Syrians constituting the largest share of arrivals in Italy in 2014. The deteriorating security situation in Libya, has also increased migration pressures.

Estimates of numbers of sub-Saharan migrants who die while trying to reach Northern Africa are very hazy. According to the blog Fortress Europe, from 1996 to 2014, at least 1,790 migrants have perished crossing the Sahara. It is acknowledged that this underestimates the true number. Data compiled by IOM suggest only 1.4 per cent of deaths in the first nine months of 2014, occurred in the Sahara. However, this estimate is hampered by lack of available data and certainly does not include all the lives lost through migration in the region. Testimonies of migrants who have journeyed through the Sahara indicate the certain prevalence of death along this route. About 195 migrants have been known to die or go missing while making the crossing from 2010 to 2013 (UNHCR, 2013). The numbers for 2014 were up considerably from 2012 and 2013.

On October 3rd, 2013, over 360 people lost their lives travelling from Libya to Lampedusa, Italy, when their boat sank just a quarter-mile from its destination. With roughly 500 passengers jammed into a 20-metre-long boat, efforts to attract attention following engine trouble led to a fire that engulfed the ship in flames. Survivors tell horrifying stories of hours spent at sea as their companions died around them. A second shipwreck, near Lampedusa, later in the month, resulted in another 34 deaths. While these events are tragic and alarming, they are not isolated incidents. IOM estimates that between January and September

2014, at least 4,077 migrants died attempting to reach destinations around the world. This figure, largely driven by increases in the

Mediterranean region, is nearly 70 per cent higher than the 2,400 deaths recorded for the whole of 2013.

Since year 2000, IOM estimates that at least 40,000 migrants have died.

While significant, these global figures still fail to capture the true number of fatalities. Many migrant deaths occur in remote regions of the world and are never recorded. In some cases, boats, and all their passengers disappear at sea and no deaths are reported. Some experts estimate that for every dead body found on the shores of the developed world, there are at least two others that are never recovered (Weber and Pickering, 2011).

Data on the number of migrant deaths is sketchy, and in some areas almost non-existent. The vast majority of governments do not publish number of deaths because counting the lives lost is largely left to civil society and the media.

According to the IOM, as of November 20th 2015, there have been 954,456 migrant arrivals by sea in Europe in 2015. 5,113 died or are missing. Greece and Italy has the highest arrivals at 699,457 and 142,484 respectively. The majority of the deaths at 3,695 occurred in the Mediterranean. The number of Arrivals in Italy was 3,528 in January, but has now cumulatively reached 150,317 in December.

The figures cumulatively for arrivals in Italy are:

JAN	FEB	MAR	APR	MAY	JUN
3,528	7,882	10,165	26,228	47,449	70,354

JUL	AUG	SEP	OCT	NOV
93,540	116,147	132,069	140,636	142,484

The top five countries with Italy as the destination are:

ERITERIA	NIGERIA	SOMALIA	SUDAN	SYRIA
37,796	19,576	11,020	8,692	7,232

There were 3,166 deaths in the Mediterranean recorded in 2014 and as of November 2015, there are 3,695 in the same region. July was the worst month in 2014, with 864 deaths. April's has been the worst in 2015 with 1244.

The deaths by region as of December 18th 2015 are as follows:

Mediterranean	3,695
South East Asia	736
Horn of Africa	94
Sahara and North Africa	85
Sub Saharan Africa	40

All numbers are estimates based on data from respective governments and IOM field offices.

"We know how many people arrive in Italy, but we will never know how many people actually depart Libya. We think there are shipwrecks that remain unknown and unfortunately the total of 3695 recorded deaths (Jan-Dec 18 2015) in the Mediterranean is probably an underestimation", said Flávio Di Giacomo, an IOM spokesperson in Italy.

As of October 26th 2015, 7513 migrants had arrived in Italy in just that month alone. In 2014, 15,279 landed in Italy in October. The decline could be attributed to the fact that Syrians are now entering Europe through Greece. Excluding the Syrians, the number of arrivals has increased compared to 2014. Since the beginning of the year, the total number of sea arrivals in Greece has exceeded 550,000. IOM reports that approximately 160,000 migrants and refugees crossed into Greece from Turkey in October.

Despite worsening weather conditions, IOM staff say that the number of arrivals continued to be high. For areas where the IOM is present, the arrivals by sea to Italy for Gambians in 2014 and 2015 were 6,179 and 6,315 respectively.

In 2014, as a foreword to the report "Fatal Journeys Tracking Lives Lost

During Migration" William Lacy Swing, Director General of the IOM said the following.

"One year ago (2013), the world watched in horror when some 360 migrants lost their lives in the attempt to swim to the shores of the Italian island of Lampedusa. Regrettably, the horror seems endless: up to 500 migrants met their death at sea off Malta just a few weeks before this report was published. Two survivors reported that smugglers deliberately rammed and sunk their ship when migrants refused to board a less seaworthy vessel, after having been forced to switch boats at sea many times on their journey from Egypt. Two weeks after the incident, there were only 11 identified survivors; witnesses reported that as many as 100 children were on board.

These tragedies in the Mediterranean are but two examples of the many migrant tragedies unfolding all over the world. Hundreds perish every year on the journey from Central America to the United States through Mexico, under the desert sun or robbed and beaten along the way; migrants drown on their way from Indonesia to Australia, or off the coast of Thailand and in the Bay of Bengal; migrants die of thirst crossing the Sahara Desert into North Africa, or drown in the Gulf of Aden as they try to reach the Middle East. In many of these cases migrants often disappear and die without a trace. The paradox is that at a time when one in seven people around the world are migrants in one form or another, we are seeing a harsh response to migration in the developed world. Limited opportunities for safe and regular migration drives would-be migrants into the hands of smugglers, feeding an unscrupulous trade that threatens the lives of desperate people. We need to put an end to this cycle. Undocumented migrants are not criminals, but human beings in need of protection and assistance, entitled to legal assistance, and deserving respect. I have repeatedly emphasized the need for smarter policies to end the horror of migrant deaths, and particularly "practical protection" measures to guarantee safe and regular ways for migrants to reach their destinations". Collecting and presenting information about who these migrants are, where they come from and why they move is the first indispensable step to understanding this global tragedy and designing evidence-based, effective policy responses and practical protection measures to prevent further loss of life. In providing the first global count of migrant fatalities and recommendations for better data collection, this report aims to catalyze a prompt and unified response from all parties concerned with this tragedy – governments, international organizations, civil society, companies and the scholarly community. The time is now, and we are already late"

CHAPTER 12

With the humanitarian flag raised, the Triton replacing the Mare Nostrum and Italy going to the rescue of all these migrants at sea, one can't help but wonder why. The Italian rescue mission paradoxically, may be encouraging more migrants to risk everything in these undoubtedly ill-equipped boats. Looking from the outside one wonders why is Italy so inviting. It seems like an encouragement and an enticement for migrants to continue to try this journey across the Mediterranean. "All" one has to do is cross the Mediterranean and you are all set. What does Italy or Europe as a whole have to gain from this migration? If all ships arriving from Libya were turned back, would this mass exodus continue? If the folks rescued were sent back to their native lands, would we see a decrease in the number of folks trying to embark on this potentially fatal journey? Even for those who make it, the reality of life in Europe as an asylum seeker or economic migrant is likely to prove crushing. For some, the odyssey will come full circle and they will go back home defeated. It has become distinctively clear that Italy cannot handle the number of migrants entering the country.

There are reports that Italy Is Allowing Migrants who survive the voyage to 'disappear' into Europe. It is thought that the Italian Navy saved some 170,000 boat people in 2014 and brought them to Italy. It is also thought, that Italy's Centre-Left government then lost all trace of 100,000 of them once inside Italy. There have been persistent reports in Italy of police dumping coachloads of migrants at railway stations such as Milan and Rome in the hope that they would voluntarily leave Italy. It does not matter where they come from, be it Senegal or The Gambia, they are all called migrants. For so many, it becomes a reality to actually make it only to find that Europe does not want them.

A "Back Wayer" made a comment that "all you have to do is make it to Italy because they cannot send you back." "Even if your "Asylum" case does not get granted", he went on to say, "you will not be deported as all you have to do is appeal". Almost all appeal cases are won and if not, there are other avenues. Everyone who is not granted asylum is deported – in theory. But that is not what happens. Few of those handed deportation papers leave. They just disappear. And when those without papers refuse to tell the authorities their name and country of origin, Italy has no idea where to send them. In 2013, approximately 40,000 deportation papers were issued but only some 5,000 migrants actually left Italy. Fabrizio Gatti, a L'Espresso journalist who is an expert on the migrant issue, says: "Literally dozens of these foreigners are lost at all hours of the day and night. Rescued at sea and counted, once ashore they've just been left free to abscond." According to Andrea Maestri, a Ravenna-based asylum lawyer, the authorities actively collaborate in such absconding. "The police did this quite openly last year and no doubt they will do it again this year, too, in the summer when the wheel really flies off," says Maestri. "All you had to do was go to Milan station and watch the coaches pull up."

While the transatlantic slave trade shipped large numbers of Africans to the West from the sixteenth to the nineteenth century, significant voluntary migration to the west started in the eighties. Traders initially sent slaves to Europe to work as servants until the market for labor expanded in the West Indies and North America in the eighteenth century. In 1807, the United Kingdom abolished the slave trade throughout its empire. It also tried, unsuccessfully, to end the slave trade in The Gambia. Slave ships intercepted by the Royal Navy's West Africa Squadron in the Atlantic were also returned to The Gambia, with liberated slaves released on McCarthy Island far up The Gambia River where they were expected to establish new lives.

Those that are campaigning against the "Back Way" find it hard to understand why any human being would subject himself to such a treacherous journey. Those that take on the journey or sympathetic to the cause will argue that the lack of prospects of a decent life can force one to embark on this journey. A good number of people all over the world cannot understand the "get rich or die trying" phenomenon. The belief that success has to happen overnight continues to plague the minds of many Gambians. Almost every success story you hear started several years back, sometimes decades.

This "Back Way" journey has devastated so many lives, albeit, a few having been changed for the better. The focus continues to be on individual success while losing sight of the fact that there are alternatives, as few as they may be. A valid question to pose would be whether the efforts, time, money and dedication invested on this treacherous journey could be better spent on creating and searching for opportunities in The Gambia? Are those living in the diaspora spending time educating folks back home about the diaspora and what to expect?

Understanding the realities of what lies ahead in any journey for greener pastures, goes a long way in determining success.

Arguably, the reason for embarking on this journey is that of economic situation and not persecution for most Gambians. The saying that 'desperate times call for desperate measures' comes to mind as one tries to answer questions as to why anyone embarks on this often fatal journey. No one has the answers to all these questions and without being in the shoes of the "Back Wayer", the attempt to understand his plight is simply that; an attempt.

So many "Back Wayers" reach their "dreamland" [Italy] only to realize that it was simply that; a dream or a nightmare even!

Below is a speech about the migration issues, from Matteo Renzi, prime minister of Italy.

"The search for peace and food that is forcing thousands of women and men, often with their young children in tow, to risk their lives reaching Europe didn't begin today, and it won't end tomorrow. Anyone who thinks this crisis can be solved with a tweet or a Facebook post lives in a parallel universe.

The history of humanity has been marked by migration flows, but it is fear that allows shallow demagoguery, and sometimes open racism, increasingly to inhabit Europe's politics – to the extent that it has been the decisive factor in several recent elections.

The country I represent, Italy, has saved countless human lives over the past months. I'd like to pay tribute to the women and men, both military and civilian, who even now are displaying solidarity and courage in keeping our fellow human beings alive. Aboard the ships of our navy and coastguard, three babies have been born in the past six months.

These "angels of the sea" are making Europe a better place. I used to be the mayor of Florence. The identity of this great region stems from the masterpieces of past geniuses, from Michelangelo to Leonardo, from Galileo to Brunelleschi, from the Uffizi to the Palazzo Vecchio. But when I used to speak to elderly people in cafes or in the streets, they would tell me that the thing they were proudest of wasn't the ancient masterpieces, but having helped to save lives and protect artworks during the flood of 1966.

We used to call these people the "angels of the mud". Today, Italy is proud of its angels of the sea, just as Florence was of its angels of the mud.

However, while lives are being saved we also know that there isn't enough room for everyone. Whoever has the right to asylum must be welcome in Europe, not just in Italy, despite the EU's Dublin regime. But it is inconceivable that one country should tackle the entirety of this problem on its own. Responsibility and solidarity are concepts that go hand in hand.

Anyone who doesn't have the right to remain in Europe must be repatriated. And in those countries, the European Union – including Italy – must do more in terms of providing aid, to support international development projects, and cultural and technological exchange programmes.

But Europe must have a strategy. And it needs to be clear. Today's uncertainty will lead to tomorrow's problems. This is what happened in Libya, where intervention put an end to a brutal dictatorship, but that intervention wasn't followed up with a strategy to deal with the aftermath. We are, as a consequence, now paying the price of this failure. More than 90% of migrants to Italy leave from a Libyan coast that is no longer guarded by the government.

Today's problem isn't about Italy facing this emergency alone. We're a great country that will not fall into hysteria just because one year we have a few thousand more refugees than expected. If forced to do it alone, we would not shy away from the challenge. We will not stop saving lives, because on our shoulders we have centuries of civilization. We will not turn our backs on that just to improve our ratings in the opinion polls: human life matters more than approval.

However, an EU-wide response is needed by Europe far more than it is needed by Italy. Italy could go it alone in the Mediterranean. But it's Europe that cannot afford to let this happen. That's the political point. It's Europe that needs to demonstrate the values it believes in and stands for. Europe isn't a bundle of economic ties, it's a community of people, a shared destiny, and ideals. If this common purpose is diminished, we lose our European identity.

If selfishness and fear prevail, we risk losing the noble idea underpinning the European project

We want to fight for a set of values, for civility and peace. This is why the European Union was founded – not for bond spreads and stability pacts, but for these values."

CHAPTER 13

Millions of people all over the world have been displaced by war, oppression and economic hardships. This current migrant crisis is the worst since World War II. It has been in effect for quite some time. However the recent conflicts in countries have only made the situation worse. This has led to migration in huge numbers, often risking lives along the way.

Afghans and Syrians make up the vast majority of the migrants. They are fleeing wars in their respective countries; wars that continue to get brutal daily. In Syria where ISIS (Islamic State of Iraq and Levant) has created Chaos along with the over 5 years of civil war, over 12 million have been displaced. Most of those that flee end up in Turkey, Lebanon and Jordan with an ultimate goal of making it to Europe.

In Nigeria, due to Boko Horam, an Islamic extremist group based in northeastern part of the country, several Nigerians are left with no choice but to flee. Same goes for Afghanistan, Kosovo and Eritrea. The primary reason for leaving these countries is civil unrest. The migrations occur in extremely dangerous conditions. Africans pay huge sums of money to embark on these journeys. A lot of them do not even make it to the boats because of kidnapping, rape and torture in an effort to extort more money from them. Africans' main destination in Europe is usually Italy or Greece.

This migration, the journey to Europe is an expensive one-both financially and in regards to safety. It is a very difficult journey and casualties are not uncommon. Despite all the uncertainties and dangers associated with this journey, families continue to embark on it in search of better lives. All these migrants consider Europe as the only option out of their current predicaments. The EU is divided on how to handle the migrant crisis. A few nations are not welcoming the migrants with open arms, quite understandably. Italy and Greece has seen overwhelming arrivals and naturally has put a constraint in their already rocky economic situations. For so many of these migrants, their ultimate goal is to reach affluent European countries. However this journey requires going through countries that are no so welcoming. In Hungary, a razor wire fence was built to deter migrants from entering the country. The situation is made more difficulty by the confusion between a refugee and a migrant. Migrant generally refers to all those people arriving in Europe overall. It's worth noting that there is a legal difference between the two.

With Eriteria and Nigeria as exceptions, most of those arriving from Africa left their countries in search of better economic opportunities- they are regular migrants. They would not qualify for Asylum and have to go through the normal immigration process. Refugees are those that have been forced out of their countries due to war and civil unrest and are eligible for asylum. The Asylum process is usually a lengthy one that can take up to two years. Germany has suspended the Dublin regulation and anticipates receiving over 800,000 refugees and asylum seekers in 2015. Germany, France and Sweden are urging other member states to share the refugee burden with mandatory quotas. Naturally other countries object wanting to maintain control over the number of refugees they can accept.

There is not a clear path to handle the migrant crisis- help, if forthcoming is several months or years away.

A single news coverage will do a huge injustice to the migrant crisis. All the migrants come from different countries and all have different stories to tell. They enter so many different European countries- countries that have their own laws regarding asylum.

Sadly-The migrant crisis continues.

The unanimous conclusion is that every human life is as precious as the next. Furthermore, the migrants need help and protection.

If one life is saved from this book, a mission would have been accomplished. The life you save by reading this book could be your own.

The proceeds from this book will help in creating opportunities for youths primarily in The Gambia and get them to better understand the "Back Way".

www.ingramcontent.com/pod-product-compliance
Lightning Source LLC
Chambersburg PA
CBHW021544290526
45785CB00004BA/1504